A Vessel
Made Ready

D1205598

A VESSEL
MADE READY

Wendy Winans

A VESSEL
MADE READY

Printed in the United States of America
ISBN-13: 978-0578496573

Author Contact:
Wendy Winans
wendywinans1968@gmail.com

Book Reviews

"This is an awesome book by any standard. The author paints vivid word pictures, beginning with her first encounter with Christ at a very young age, continuing to show Himself real in the world about her, throughout her life. I am happy to have been allowed to read this work prior to its publication."

- Harry Oglesby
Pipe Insulator/LPN - Baton Rouge, Louisiana

"The first chapter was my favorite. I saw Jesus too. He showed me the waters in His eyes. They were blue, and like waves. He is very beautiful. And you shall seek me, and find me, when you shall search for me with all your heart (Jer. 29:13)."

-Debra Oglesby
Homemaker - Baton Rouge, Louisiana

"This book is a powerhouse of encouragements. Wendy wrote with such passion, embracing every page with the refining process of our lives. The fiery furnace in the path of her career and life will definitely be a comfort to all who read this book. All will be challenged and rewarded with a peaceful assurance "Jesus loves me.""

-Sharlyn Metcalf
Flight Attendant - Deer Lodge, Montana

Dedication

*I would like to dedicate this book
to Jesus Christ, my first love.
Lord You are my Savior and
my Redeemer. Apart from
You there would have
been no book. To You
be all the Glory, Honor and Praise!!!*

Acknowledgements

Mom and Dad, thank you for everything. You are amazing! Beau, what can I say, but that you are the best brother any sister could have. I love you all.

Harry and Debra Oglesby. I have found your friendship to be faithful. How rare!

Monique Piper, thank you for your contribution towards the editing phase of this work. You have been a great help.

Sarah P. Allemand, your ability to see error is truly a God given gift, and the heart you have showed towards this work will not be forgotten.

Timothy Piper, I appreciate you working with the cover. Beautiful!

Thank You!

Table of Contents

Introduction

A t the risk of veering off the orthodox path of traditional writing, I would like for you to walk with me to the edge of the bank, and like a pebble that skips across the waters, so will our journey be as we move to certain areas of my time in the furnace; that you may be comforted concerning your own seasonal fires (2 Cor. 1:3-4). Our limited view regarding our painful pilgrimage here seems to fan the flames of our sufferings at times. Surely, we have not always understood why the Lord would allow so much pain in our lives; and secretly, we are hurt with Him because of it. Although the Lord moves to lift our head from a place of discouragement, we are reluctant in our response because we have not understood His ways.

For a period of twelve years, I worked in the piping industry. The first five years I worked for some of our more prestigious companies within the field. However, the following seven the Lord moved some things around and I found myself at a small family owned business. This change in career direction of course made no sense; that is until I realized what God was teaching me concerning our afflictions. I would like to share with you some of what I discovered, both in our natural life along with our supernatural life; as well as my journey through what I have labeled the "furnace" period of my life, in hopes to bring a little understanding your way.

Please let me say, precious one, that your Father in Heaven has a love for you that can in no wise be comprehended with the natural mind. I am writing you for this very reason. It is my hope that by the time you reach the end of this book, you will fling the doors of your heart open toward the Maker of your soul and say, "Lord forgive me for my distance, it's making more sense now!"

This book you are holding is my hand. I have come to get you for a journey that we may hike through the rocky terrains of my adversities, skip over to my valleys of no answers, take a rest by the flowing streams of a refreshing word. At the last, we will scale the mountains for a higher view until we reach the place of Gods' perspective. Seeing our afflictions through His eyes has a way of readjusting our perception, thus alleviating a great portion of our pain.

Ok now, let's gear up and put our traveling clothes on. We have a little ground to cover. Take hold of that flash light you have there, you will need this as we wade through the dark tunnels of a despairing moment. Next, you will need a good pair of trekking boots for the rocky places that may stub your belief system. Make sure your ropes are good and sturdy; you may need something to hold onto when your mind is stretched to consider the Jesus I know. Be sure to pack your swimming gear; we might hit some tumultuous seas, so we'll need to be prepared for that. Now, about those britches, make sure they have some pockets because you may find a pearl or two along the way. I think this just about does it. Are you ready? Wonderful, let's get started! Oh, by the way, my friend, reach over and grab that tin cup you have there because our first stop will be at The Fountain. We will need plenty of nourishment for our journey. Ready? Let's go! Don't forget your cup!

Chapter One

The Fountain

———⚜———

For God, who commanded the light to shine out of darkness, hath shined in our hearts, to give the light of the knowledge of the glory of God in the face of Jesus Christ. (2 Cor. 4:6)

Psst! Did you bring your cup? Good! Oh, get your rope out, I have a feeling you just might need it. Around the age of four, I can clearly remember my mother bringing me and my younger brother to church. Oh, how I loved going to church because it always seemed to be some sort of celebration. There was just so much joy. The people would laugh, dance, play tambourines and sing about a man named Jesus. I did not know this man Jesus, but everyone else sure seemed to know Him. Week after week, we would go to church, and I would watch the people behave in a way I did not understand. As I would look about the sanctuary, hands would lift, tears would fall, and their faces seemed to have a light about them. I wondered why we were not like this at home. Furthermore, I would ponder, "Who is this man Jesus, they keep singing songs about?"

As the people would worship, the atmosphere would fill with an exhilarating joy. There was a sense of liveliness that would make you forget every sorrow. Each time we went to church, it was this same wonderful experience which brought about a desire in my heart to know more about the one they called Jesus. I would think, "This man Jesus is famous. He must have really done something for us because everybody sure seems to like Him around here. Oh well, I might as well join in the fun." So, I would grab my tambourine and dance up and down the aisles. My, what joy! I loved coming to church. It was my favorite thing to do.

Returning home felt quite different than the joy of being in church as we all struggled through various trials. However, no matter our difficulties, my desire to know Jesus seemed to be greater than anything else in my life. Thoughts of what He might be like consumed me. My imagination would dance about with excitement anticipating the day that I would get to meet the famous man, Jesus. My desire to know Him was growing, and I knew I would not be satisfied until I met Him. The first time my ears heard the sound of His name, I was taken captive. Every time Momma took us to the church house, I went inside and started looking around for Him.

Everybody seemed to know Jesus. That's why He was famous to me. And what do famous people do? They get on stage in front of everybody. As the people would sing, I would hear them say the name of Jesus. This to me was calling on Him to come and be with us. So, when the people would start calling Jesus, I would bend over looking down the aisle, waiting for Him to come out and get on that stage. Over and over I looked for Him, but never would I see Him come. I did not understand why Jesus would not come to church so we could be with Him. We kept calling Him by His name, but He does not come. This did not make much sense to me because when Momma called my name, that meant I had to pay attention; stop playing around and come see what Momma wanted. If I did not come when my name was called, well then, that spelled trouble.

I thought to myself that maybe Jesus wasn't paying attention to His name being called, or maybe He just couldn't hear us. Either way, I was thinking that Jesus could get into trouble one day. The big people's world did not make much sense to me anyway. So, I just decided to let it go for the time being. However, as time went on and we continued going to church, my desire to meet Jesus would not leave me. On the contrary, it was increasing all the more until I became frustrated about the entire matter. I could not figure out for the life of me, why no one would take me to meet Him. I had it in my mind that it was the "big people's" job to take us "little ones" to meet Him; and if they will not, who will? I began to think that if someone could just drive me to His house, then I would go knock on His door myself. No one would have to do anything for me; I would do it all by myself if they could just get me there.

Finally, my desire to meet Jesus became so heavy I just could not carry it anymore. Hoping that Jesus could hear me somehow I began talking into the air, "Jesus, nobody will take me to meet you, and I don't know how to find You. I know one day I will get to meet you and when I do, I am going to be the first one to tell you how famous you are. Everybody loves You down here. The people dance about and sing songs with your name in it. Oh! and it's important for You to know who I am. My name is Wendy, and I play the tambourine for You."

Somehow, I felt light again. I just knew Jesus would make a way for me to meet Him some day. I did not know when or how; but, I knew Jesus would find a way, and I was satisfied to wait my turn. Until then, I decided that I would keep on dancing, singing and playing my tambourine because it was just so much fun. Besides this, the Preacher Man still taught us about Jesus, and I knew this would have to do until my big day.

Meanwhile, our journey at home was filled with a variety of adjustments as my younger brother and I endured the separation of our parents. But no matter what size our problems were, my hope of meeting Jesus one day was bigger than any sorrow. Now, at the age of six, I was still learning how to adjust to our new life. Momma was still mindful to get me and my little brother to the church house, so we could keep learning about Jesus. My thoughts of Jesus were sustaining me and keeping my hope alive.

One day, Momma loaded us up in the car for a trip to the grocery store. Arriving back home and knowing the routine, I climbed out and headed toward the trunk of the car to give Momma a hand. When all of a sudden, I felt someone take hold of me. They turned me in the direction of our apartment and instructed me to go inside. I looked around to see who it was, but I could not see them. This was very strange I thought. Not being able to make sense of it, I shook if off and turned back toward Momma's direction. Again, I was taken hold of, but this time, I could feel His authority. I knew it was important for me to listen, so I left right away. The "Presence" was very pleasant, and I was not afraid. But as I followed Him, I did wonder where He was taking me. I also considered it strange, that Momma was not hollering at me, to get back over there and help her with the groceries. I thought maybe He had a talk with Momma, and she said it was ok for Him to take me. I did not know!

Reaching the door of our apartment, I stepped inside. The "Presence" released me and somehow, I felt as though He wanted me to see something. I turned my head to look about the room, searching for anything that would make sense to me. When my eyes landed on our icebox (refrigerator) in the kitchen, I heard the words, "Go open the door!" This felt like the biggest "hide-and-go-seek" game yet; and, I was excited! Curious to see what was on the other side of that door, I walked over, pushed the big silver handle upward and pulled the big door open. The first thing I saw was a plain ole light bulb. The same one that's always in the icebox. But this time, the light was different. This Light was a brilliant white, and its brightness was so intense, until I was not sure how my eyes were able to bear such a Light. I felt such a great comfort as though I were being bathed in light.

As I am trying to understand this unusual Light, a very beautiful face comes out from the Light. I said, "My goodness, aren't you cold in there?" The "Man in The Light" did not answer, but I could tell by His smile that He was a very happy Man. Beams of light were shining through His face. They were so bright until I could barely see His features. The Man continues to smile, as though He was waiting for something. So, I just stood still and studied Him. I began to feel a slow saturation of joy fill me as I realized who this smiling Man was. It's the one they call Jesus, but "My heaven's, what is Jesus doing in the icebox?"

A current of joy began to storm through me until the shout hit the doors of my lips, "It's Jesus! It's Jesus! It's Jesus! He has found me! He has found me! Even when I could not find Him. He made a way for me. Jesus has found me." After the mouth had its turn, joy hit my arms and they flew in the air. After the arms, my stomach got tickled and I was bent in laughter. Then, joy found the kneecaps, and they went to vibrating. When joy made its way to my feet, I shot across the floor in a wild display of adoration that must have shook everything around me. I could see Jesus laughing at my shouting and dancing about as He watched me lose myself in His presence. I was plum wild in my dance before Him. He knew I had been waiting to see Him. Joy went to every part of me until I was filled from head to toe. How true it is that our joy is made full in His presence (Psalm 16:11).

I continued my dancing and shouting until I out right wore myself down. Catching my breath: I shouted, "Jesus, You are famous! We love You! We sing songs about You down here! We dance for You. Oh! and my name is Wendy; I play the tambourine for You!" After I got all of this out, my surroundings faded, and I found myself suspended in His glorious light. Then Jesus said, "I am about to put you inside of Me." I did not understand His words, but at His will, I could feel myself being drawn in His direction.

His light shined right through His skin, and it was so extreme until I could only see portions of His face. However, the closer He drew me in, the more I could see. When His face came into full view, I lost my breath at His beauty, my understanding left me, and my ability to move was no more. His eyes teemed with eternal realties and an everlasting beauty that is of a supernatural nature. He drew me even closer to His face, and I watched His eyeballs slowly disappear until I could see blue waves of waters in both of His eyes. Jesus said, "You are looking at the Living Waters." As I stood looking at these waters, I could feel the nourishment of life filling me. Jesus drew me in closer again; and then closer, and then closer until I passed right through His face and into His body. Once I was inside of Him, I turned to look in every direction until I saw a path filled with Light. I walked over to have a look and to see where it would lead me, if I chose to walk on it. I bent over for a closer look and noticed how narrow this path was. I looked as far as I was able trying to find the end of it, but there was no end. I understood that I was looking into eternity. This is when I realized Jesus, Himself, was eternal and He had no end.

You will show me the Path of Life: in Your Presence is fullness of joy; at Your right hand there are pleasures for evermore.
(Psalms 16:11)

How excellent is thy lovingkindness, O God! therefore, the children of men put their trust under the shadow of thy wings. They shall be abundantly satisfied with the fatness of thy house; and thou shalt make them drink of

the river of thy pleasures. For with thee is the
fountain of life in thy light shall we see light.
(Psalm 36:7-9)

Jesus speaks again, "This will be the path that you will walk." The next thing I know I am back on the ground, looking up in His direction. Jesus said, "I knew you before you were born. Your life here is temporary." I responded, "But we have never met before. How could You know me before I was born? If this be so, then where was I before I came here?" I knew Jesus understood me, but He gave no answer. He just continued to look upon me with a great love.

Jesus continued looking on me as though He was pleased with me somehow. So, I said, "Lord, why are You so pleased with me? I am only a little girl; I am not big enough to do anything good yet." Jesus did not answer this question either. But all of a sudden, I saw power come out from Him in the form of Love, Joy and Peace. All three lively forms moved in my direction, until I was surrounded and submerged by all that Christ is. I thought, "Oh my! I like the way Jesus gives hugs." Jesus then looked at me with a fun, half-like smile, along with a mysterious squint in His eyes that said, "I know something you don't." A flame of fire ignited, and I was set on fire for Jesus right there. I could feel waves of fire wash over me; stirring up an endless passion, hunger and thirst to know Him more. Jesus knew right well how to set me ablaze. The very thought of Him knowing something I didn't started my chase after Him. I knew that I would never see the same again, and that I would spend the remainder of my life searching Him out.

As I am staring into Him, I begin thinking, "Oh my heavens! Momma needs to see Jesus." Keeping a good stern eye on Jesus to make sure He didn't get away, I began hollering for Momma. I did not stop until I heard the "pitter-patter" of her feet heading in our direction. As Momma was getting closer, Jesus began to smile as if to say goodbye. In His eyes I could see His love for me. My heart could feel a painful tug for Him not to leave. As Momma came closer, Jesus faded back into the light. Oh! How my heart began to ache as I watched Him leave. My yearning to go with Him was nearly overwhelming. How I wished I had not said anything, then I could have kept Him a little longer.

My mother never got to see Jesus that day, but I had no problem filling her in on all the details and anyone else who could stand to listen to me, for that matter. I have been telling others of this personal meeting with Jesus my entire life. Now, more than forty years later, my meeting with Him has not diminished but remains new. That was the day I met the One who loved me first. The love of Jesus is perfectly pure and is a living power. When Jesus hugs us, He wraps all that He is around us and His amazing love goes right through your being. Life in the spirit is so much fun! How incredible it is that our spirit can commune with His Spirit in such an effortless way. All we had to do was think thoughts, and we were talking. So easy! There is absolutely no compulsion to use the mouth. I discovered that it was more natural to talk in this manner, than what we do here on earth.

Jesus transformed my understanding and fixed my eyes, heart and mind on eternal matters. His reality, power and presence will completely alter your perception of what you think is real. It is amazing to be in His presence, because you just start knowing things. Revelation just pours inside of you, and it's the kind of knowledge that's only known by way of intimacy and cannot be learned any other way, nor is there an expression for it (Jer. 33:3). He is a Living Power. To be in His Presence is enough. It is impossible to encounter our Creator face to face and not be altered in some way. I often wondered throughout my life why Jesus chose this way to introduce Himself. I have not figured it out to this day; but this I know, Jesus is no mere man! He can do whatever He pleases. He has no limits. Maybe Jesus wanted me to know that He was no ordinary man, and that He has the power to do anything. Well, I am convinced in a forever kind of way.

Jesus showed me that He had no limits when He could manifest inside of a refrigerator and then out from the light bulb. This right here told me that Jesus could live where no man could live and do what no man could do. I understood that Jesus had the ability to show up whenever He wanted to, wherever He wanted to; and communicate with us in whichever way He chooses to.

Jesus is everywhere and in everything. He fills all things, and in Him are all things (Eph. 4:10, Col. 1:17, 1John 5:11, 5:20). I learned at six-years old that I would never go anywhere in this life that Jesus couldn't find me, because He was in me and I was in Him. Literally! I did not know it then, but now that I am older, I understand that I was baptized into Jesus Christ that day.

*For ye are all the children of God by faith in Christ
Jesus. For as many of you have been baptized into
Christ have put on Christ.
(Gal. 3:26-27)*

Eternity is inside of Jesus, just as I saw it was. Everything that emanates from Him is alive and moves with power. The Love, Joy and Peace that came out of Him have a life form about them and they were moving. Jesus can give us a peace that surpasses all understanding because Peace is alive. It's not just a feeling. Peace lives!

*And this is the record, that God has given to us
Eternal Life, and this life is in His Son.*
(1 John 5:11)

*And the peace of God, which passeth all
understanding, shall keep your hearts
and minds through Christ Jesus.
(Phil. 4:7)*

Chapter Two

Groom Road

————————⚜————————

Many are the afflictions of the righteous:
But the Lord delivers him out of them all.
He keeps all his bones: not one of them
Is broken.
(Psalm 34:19-20)

How did you enjoy meeting my Jesus? Wonderful, is He not? This was indeed a mountain top experience. Now, we head to the valley, so fasten your boots and keep your flashlight handy. There's a dark tunnel just up ahead. I would like to highlight a few particulars of my first trial, that you may see what I gained.

Shortly after meeting Jesus and turning seven years of age, my Mother was approached in church with an offer of help, due to our desperate need. As some stories go, our Mother was single and trying to provide for two children. With the threat of going under, we were forced to accept the offer and moved in with a family of seven: a traveling preacher, his wife and their five children. My younger brother and I, of course, were excited at the prospect of our new playmates.

Our life became something altogether different as the three of us were divided with various schedules. My baby brother was only four years old, but I went to school and did not return until around three in the afternoon. Our mother worked from three to eleven and did not come home until almost midnight. For nearly two years, we saw our mother in passing only. Point being, we were left in the care of the Preacher Man, as I refer to him.

Each day, my Mother headed off to work convinced all was well with me and my younger brother. Oh, how I wish that had been true, but the beatings and various things he would do to make us afraid became more intense and frequent as time went on. I could not understand the Preacher Man's behavior. Why did he hate us? We were only children. The big people were supposed to be nice to us, I thought. No matter the case, I just knew my Jesus was seeing every bit of it, and He was going to show up any minute and take us away from this mean ole man.

Late one night, when the Preacher Man thought I was asleep, I overheard him use the word "hate" to describe his feelings for me. It was difficult for me to understand how an adult could feel this way toward a child. I began to weep quietly because up until that moment I had only known love by those around me. Every child just naturally believes that everyone loves them. However, I could feel the Preacher Man's hatred in every beating. I was beaten with whatever was within his reach until my body was bruised with bloody slashes. I just knew he was going to end up breaking something one day, but not a bone was broken. On another occasion, around midnight, when all were asleep, I felt the harsh blow of an angry hand take hold of me. I was jerked out of bed, drug through the house, out the back door, and through the pasture until he was satisfied we were far enough away so no one could hear. The beating, itself, I have little memory of, to which I am grateful. I slept with one eye open after that.

Finding places to weep, my thoughts would turn toward Jesus and His whereabouts. I wondered where my Jesus was and why He was not coming for me. I knew He could see me. Surely, He knows where I am! Where was He? Furthermore, why am I hated so much? I am only a little girl. What kind of world did Jesus put me in for goodness sake?

Still waiting for my answers, I found myself in the living room one evening listening to the Preacher Man discussing a certain address with his children. Maybe somewhere else to preach or something. I did not know, but everyone seemed to be in a good mood, and I wanted so much to make friends with them, so we could all be happy and at peace. So, I playfully picked an address out of thin air and suggested they could drive to street 4311. Suddenly, their voices rose in anger, claiming that I told them to go to hell. I thought, "What is hell?" Before I had a chance to figure out what was wrong, they stormed in my direction yelling that 4311 is hell turned upside down. I did not know what to think. They began hitting me and shoving me through the house and out the front door. I thought, "What is this turned upside down mean, and how does that turn into letters?" They began pushing and shoving me down the porch as they continued their yelling. They were kicking me in the back, tossing me this way and that way down the driveway until they pushed me out into the street of oncoming traffic. The Preacher Man held me by the back of my collar, forcing me to stand in the middle of the road. My fear grew, as I watched the headlights of that car getting closer and closer. Right before the car reached me, I was jerked out of the way. I was completely petrified.

For comfort, I would go sit in my Mother's room, so I could be around her belongings and reminisce about what our lives use to be like. I would often think of my time with Jesus that day, and how beautiful He was to look at. Oh, how I wondered when it would all be over. On another day, the Preacher Man grew mad again. I was beaten and beaten until I really started to grow angry at what he was doing. It was the worst beating I had received. Being made to bathe before my Mother came home, I was instructed to wear my pajama's that had long-sleeves and long pants, so all would be kept hidden. After our Mother walked in, she headed toward the fireplace where the Preacher Man and his wife were standing. My brother and I were sitting on the fold out couch, where we normally slept. My little brother takes off running in our Mother's direction for the joy of seeing her, but I did not move for the pain and sorrow. My Mother's hugs were several pats on the back, and I knew my back would not bear it. Keeping a safe distance, however, provoked suspicion. My Mother's concern tilted her head in my direction; so, I stood up slowly and walked over to her. As I watched my Mother's arm go behind my back, I braced. As soon as she gave me her pat, my anguish buckled me at the knees, and I fell in a puddle of angry tears. The Preacher Man's threatening leer held my tongue, a suitable lie was fabricated by his wife, and all was dismissed.

My resilient spirit, however, seemed to anger the Preacher Man all the more; so, it did not take much for me to find myself in another whirlwind of trouble. On one occasion we had visitors, and their children decided to explore the Preacher Man's old truck in the backyard. After everyone left, the Preacher Man went in the backyard and saw finger prints on the windows of his truck. In his fury, he came for me and my brother. We tried to tell him we were not guilty; but, he would not hear it. So, we took the punishment for something we did not do.

Shortly after this, I was sitting in church on an empty pew, allowing my numb mind to wander, as I waited for service to start. I looked over at our pastor and watched as his son stood at the base of the platform. I assumed he must have been waiting for his turn to preach one day. I admired their sharp and clean way. They were so pleasant to look at; but, I did wonder why they were allowed to stay clean and safe, while I was becoming dirty and living in constant fear.

Pondering all that's not making sense, I begin to feel a heavy and thick blanket of filth lay right on top of me. In this moment, I received an understanding of what it was which I will share in a few moments. All the harsh words, fearful things and beatings combined could not compare to what I experienced when this perversion touched me. This was an assault that cannot be expressed. Returning home from church, I continued to ponder on this "Blanket of Filth," and the revelation that came along with it. I wondered what it could all mean.

Not long after, I endure my last beating. Forced to bathe, the warm water was a sure comfort for my aching body. As I am washing up, I began looking at the bruises and bloody stripes across my small frame, and my anger grew. I got out of the tub, wrapped the wounds and went to my Mother's room for privacy. Then I dropped my robe so Jesus could see me, and with my conflicted prayer I stormed right into a meeting with Jesus. I expressed my hurt at Him for not protecting me. I acknowledged that He was my Father, and if I was to know anything of Him, then He alone would teach me. No preachers, only Him. I was convinced that man was wicked; so, he was not the one to follow. Jesus was the greater man. He was the One who loved me; so, He would be the One to follow. It took nearly two years; but, the inclination to follow man was literally beat right out of me.

Almost immediately after this prayer, we were kicked out of this "House of Affliction." It was an abrupt move that no one understood; but, earlier that day, he had violated me in a more intimate manner. I always believed that he was in a hurry to get us out of there because he knew I was at my end with him. It was ten o'clock at night and we were put in the street. As for me, I could not have been happier. I did not care where we slept just as long as it wasn't there. Finally, we were free! I remembered my first words to Jesus when I knew it was over, "Lord, they did not destroy my faith; I still believe in you."

The "abrupt move" and the "blanket of filth" were two pieces to the puzzle that I carried in my pocket for many years. Never realizing that one day, these pieces would be the two main components to understanding how all of this would one day work for my good. The life I was learning about on earth was in no way comparable to my supernatural life with Jesus. Trying to make these two realities work together I found to be a bit puzzling. Nevertheless, there was one thing that I would never be confused about, "Jesus is Alive!"

After several years had passed, I still wondered why the Lord had allowed me to go through such a hard season as that was. It just made no sense, but no matter how difficult life was for me, Jesus would always be my reality. I would still go to church because I was made to; but, I was unwilling to lend my ear to any preacher, nor would I read my Bible. To me, the Bible was not something one could put their trust in because man wrote it. Man was corrupt. So, anything he writes would be corrupt to. Aside from this, if man could be so cruel as to damage another human being in this way, then how would he ever have any regard for the Jesus I know or listen to anything He had to say?

Learning to believe

Entering my adult years, I still struggled with my lack of faith concerning the Scriptures. I kept this to myself, seeing my Mother was a Bible teacher. I would read my Bible from time to time, because the writer talked about my Jesus. Still, I knew man was wicked, therefore it was impossible for him to write about holy matters. I just could not shake the fact that man took part in writing the Scriptures. Therefore, I could not fully trust the words I read. Eventually, I thought it was best to just stop reading the Bible altogether. I also found it rather foolish for people to blindly believe in a bunch of words no one could prove anyway. However, the Lord was aware of my private war of unbelief.

Coming home from work one day, I settled in for the evening with a good book. A little into my read, I heard a voice say, "I want you to write down the days of your life on the earth." I did not know what to think. "Could this be God speaking?" I thought. Not knowing what to do, I went to sleep. After work the next day, I headed straight to the bedroom and nestled down to relax and read for a while. Flipping through the pages to find my place, I hear the voice again. "I want you to write down the days of your life on the earth." I thought, "My heavens, I think this is the Lord talking." Not knowing what to write or what to do with His words, I went to bed without writing anything. Returning home again, I repeated my routine of preparing for a relaxing evening with the same book. After a short time of reading, the voice speaks for the third time. "I want you to write down the days of your life on the earth." Realizing this was indeed the Lord, I got up and searched for a pen and paper. I was not sure what to write; so, I just somewhat journaled about my daily activities. I spent the next two years writing and keeping a diary of sorts, but during this period I did not hear anything else from the Lord. There were no more instructions from the Lord; so, I stopped writing and continued with life as I knew it.

About three to four years later, my company transferred me which caused me to relocate to a new city. Settling in and unpacking boxes, I came across the writings the Lord asked me to pen a few years earlier which I thought had been lost through my travels. I was so excited to have found them; so, I stopped everything to sit down for a read. Combing through these writings, my focus narrowed as I grew still. I knew I could not write like this. How can it be, I thought, that my hand wrote these words; yet, I knew I was the writer of this journal. The more I read, the more I was amazed and perplexed at the same time. Reaching the last page, the voice of the Lord speaks again, "If I can cause you to write like this, I can cause men to write My Word." I have been reading my Bible ever since.

Believing in His Word was a crucial step for me in many ways. It was important to learn about my Jesus through His own words, and through the testimonies of others who had also met Him. After learning the Word, a little, the Lord wanted to give me more understanding regarding my trial with the Preacher Man. I decided to spend the night with an elderly lady to whom I was very close. The next morning, while packing my belongings, the Lord speaks, "Go by the Preacher Man's house." I thought I was to forgive; so, I began telling the Lord that I had forgiven him. "Go by the Preacher Man's house," the Lord says again. Knowing I needed to listen, I got in my car and headed in that direction. I was not sure if I remembered how to get there because it had been so long. However, I did remember the landmarks of a railroad track and a church with a steeple on it. As I'm driving, I feel the need to pay attention to the name of the street I lived on so many years before. Seeing the little church, I turned to cross the railroad tracks. Driving up the hill and over the tracks, I looked up toward the sign and to my surprise I saw the name, "Groom Rd." "Interesting name", I thought. As I am thinking on this name the Lord begins to speak, "You were being groomed on this road. That's what this street was about in your life." At these words, a flood of painful memories washed over me. In that moment, I knew without a doubt, the Lord did see what I was going through. "Then, why didn't He come for me?" I wondered.

Not understanding, I decided to walk off from the whole thing. I did not care why it happened, I just wanted to put the whole ugly thing behind me and try to forget as much as I could. Besides who can make sense of such a thing anyway. However, during this season, I would still read my Bible. After a time of healing and learning more about the Lord, I was finally ready to return to this "House of Affliction." It was my hope the Lord would help me understand how that horrendous experience had anything to do with being groomed. Something in me knew that I had to go back to "Groom Rd," and what I discovered changed my perception a bit. Would you like to take that ride with me?

Back to Groom Road

Returning to this house, it was as if I were seven years old again. I could see the beginnings of my trial and remembered how I cried out for Jesus to take all of it from me. Through reading the Scriptures, I learned that Jesus had a similar prayer in the Garden of Gethsemane at the beginning of His trial. He, too, cried out to His Father, to get Him out of what He was about to endure; yet, it was His Father's will for Him to remain where He was, for the greater purpose. Scripture reveals He prayed this more than once.

*And He went forward a little, and fell on the ground,
and prayed that, if it were possible, the hour might pass
from Him. And He said, Abba Father, all things are
possible unto thee; take away this cup from
me: nevertheless, not what I
will, but what thou wilt.
(Mark. 14:35-36)*

*And again, He went away, and prayed,
and spake the same words.
(Mark 14:39)*

Next, I remembered how I had known a loving
atmosphere before I came to the Preacher Man's house.
Learning about the Life of Jesus taught me that He also knew
a loving atmosphere before He came to our house down here
on earth - a place where He was treated with hatred as well,
without cause.

*If I had not done among them the works
which none other man did, they had not sin:
but now have they both seen and hated both
Me and my Father. But this cometh to pass,
that the word might be fulfilled that is
written in their law, they hated Me without
a cause.
(John 15:24-25)*

> *I have glorified thee on the earth: I have*
> *finished the work which thou gavest me*
> *to do. And now, O Father, glorify thou*
> *Me with thine own self with the glory*
> *which I had with thee before the*
> *World was.*
> *(John 17:4-5)*

Imagine what love Jesus must have known with His Father before we even existed! Looking at another scene, I remembered how this man came for me at midnight, dragging me through the house, out the back door and through the pasture to a place where I would be whipped. I was reminded how they came for Jesus at night, bringing their lanterns and torches to see, and how they took hold of Jesus, bound Him, and led Him away (John 18:2-13). He was mishandled and treated harshly until He reached the place where He was whipped.

> *I gave my back to the smiters, and*
> *my cheeks to them who plucked off*
> *the hair: I hid not my face from*
> *Shame and spitting.*
> *(Isaiah 50:6)*

> *Then released he Barabbas unto them;*
> *and when he had scourge Jesus, he*
> *delivered Him to be crucified.*
> *(Matt. 27:26)*

As many were astonied at thee; His
visage was so marred more than any
man, and His form more than the sons
Of men.
(Isaiah 52:14)

I recalled how my brother and I were falsely accused and took the punishment for something we did not do. The Word reveals that although Jesus was innocent, He knew something about being falsely accused and then paying for something He did not do.

Now the chief priests, and elders, and all the council,
sought false witness against Jesus, to put Him to
death; but found none: yes, though many false
witnesses came yet found they none. At the last
came two false witnesses.
(Matt. 26:59-60)

For Christ also hath once suffered for sins,
the just for the unjust, that he might bring
us to God, being put to death in the flesh,
but quickened by the Spirit.
(1 Peter 3:18)

I remembered all the times I had been beaten until I was bruised with bloody cuts. However, Jesus took a beating like no other man. Looking at the Hebrew definition for the word "smitten", we find words like beat, give wounds, strike, punish and kill. We know Jesus was beaten to death.

Here is a daunting thought: Where would we be had Jesus not been willing to endure this beating?

> *He is despised and rejected of men; a man*
> *of sorrows, and acquainted with grief: and*
> *we hid as it were our faces from Him; He*
> *was despised, and we esteemed him not.*
> *Surely, He hath borne our griefs, and*
> *carried our sorrows: yet we did esteem Him*
> *stricken, smitten of God, and afflicted. But*
> *He was wounded for our transgressions, He was*
> *bruised for our iniquities: the chastisement of*
> *our peace was upon Him: and with His stripes*
> *we are healed.*
> *(Isaiah 53:3-5)*

There were times I thought the Preacher Man would end up breaking something on me; but, as I said earlier not a bone was broken. Later in life, I was surprised to learn that with all the beatings Jesus endured, they did not break any of His bones.

> *Many are the afflictions of the righteous:*
> *but the Lord delivers him out of them all.*
> *He keeps all his bones: not one of them*
> *is broken.*
> *(Psalm 34:19-20)*

*For these things were done, that the
Scripture should be fulfilled. A bone
of Him shall not be broken.
(John 19:36)*

The Timing

I would like to share with you what I learned regarding the "abrupt move" or the timing of my release from this "house of affliction." Many times, I yearned for Jesus to come get me out, but to no avail. There was absolutely nothing I could do on my part to make this happen, no matter how desperate my pleas were or how many times I prayed. However, I did find it strange that I was abruptly released after I had enough and stormed into a meeting with Jesus. Looking at the natural, this man just wanted me out for fear of exposing him, but I knew there was something supernatural about the timing of my release. This stayed with me through the years, and I just could not shake it. I knew that my desperate prayer that day and my release from this house were connected somehow. Many times, I would recall this prayer searching for anything that would bring me understanding. I noticed my prayer was effectual and fervent. According to God's word, these are the types of prayers that avail much (James 5:16). I remembered the words I spoke that day, and how I became adamant about not following man because of his wickedness. I would only follow Jesus because He was the better Man. My word! I finally saw it! I found a place where my piece to the puzzle fit. My heart had finally turned in the direction God wanted it to go. The Lord already knew I had a change of heart, and that it was time to be released from the fires that brought this change. As for me, it took years before I would figure it out.

All of my previous prayers and crying out, He heard. Still, I remained in the furnace until my heart changed. The moment I decided not to be influenced by man, but to only follow Jesus, I was instantly released. The Lord removes us quickly the moment the change has taken place. I did not know the day would come where Jesus would use me in a prophetic way from time to time, and that I would stand in hard places, telling others what they do not wish to hear. The inclination to follow man, please man and to be influenced by man, had to be completely removed. I took beating after beating until that thing was driven out of my heart, and I was able to stand without faltering. We all take beatings in different ways, and if it is hard enough and long enough, the heart will be flushed of its wickedness and turn. There are a few scriptures that are hard to read and digest; but, after my experiences, they make sense to me.

Foolishness is bound in the heart of a child; but the rod of correction shall drive it far from him.
(Prov. 22:15)

Withhold not correction from the child: for if thou beatest him with the rod, he shall not die. Thou shalt beat him with the rod, and shalt deliver his soul from hell.
(Prov. 23:13-14)

He that spareth his rod hateth his son:
but he that loveth him chasteneth him
betimes.
(Prov. 13:24)

Chasten thy son while there is hope, and
let not thy soul spare for his crying.
(Prov. 19:18)

The thought of God actually being behind something like this may just be too much, but no matter what our beliefs are, we cannot deny that God allowed it and left us in, what we would consider to be a clear case of abuse. No matter my view of this hardship, I see the undeniable result of a heart deciding to follow Jesus and not man. In spite of all the things I still do not understand about the way I was treated, deep down there was always this knowing that God was having His way. Either way it goes, this I know, after I was convinced of man's wickedness and reached my decision to only follow Jesus, I was finally released from this "House of Affliction."

Many are the afflictions of the righteous: but the
Lord delivereth him out of them all.
(Ps. 34:19)

God's ways are higher than ours, as well as His thoughts. We do not have the understanding that God has. I think it is incredible that God can take what we would consider to be an outright disaster and turn a chaotic whirlwind of a mess into something good that will work in our favor. That's wisdom!

For my thoughts are not your thoughts,
neither are your ways my ways, saith the
Lord. For as the heavens are higher than
the earth, so are my ways higher than your
ways, and my thoughts than your thoughts.
(Isaiah 55:8-9)

And we know that all things work together
for good to them that love God, to them who
are the called according to his purpose.
(Rom. 8:28)

The Blanket of Filth

The "Blanket of Filth" was the other piece of the puzzle. Now, I would like to share with you what I learned concerning this. I mentioned earlier that I was sitting in church when I felt a thick blanket of filth lay on top of me. The moment this filth touched me, I was given the understanding that a "Blanket of Filth" was laid on top of Jesus when he was dying on the Cross. Now, this was quite the revelation because I was only eight years old. I did not know this side of Jesus or that He had died on a Cross for me yet. I only knew Jesus as The Glorious Man who had The Living Waters, and who loved me. So, I wondered why this filth would be placed on such a beautiful man. "What did He do to deserve this, I wondered?"

It is hard to explain this "Blanket of Filth." It was an abomination of the worst degree. All that I had gone through combined did not compare to this filth laying on top of me. There was a weight to this perversion. I felt like all that was clean, pure and innocent was replaced with this thick, blanket of filth. It was an assault like no other and an intimate violation.

Who His own Self bear our sins in His own body
on the tree, that we, being dead to sins, should
live unto righteousness: by whose stripes you
were healed.
(1 Peter 2:24)

All we like sheep have gone astray; we have
turned everyone to his own way; and the
Lord has laid on Him the iniquity of us all.
(Isaiah 53:6)

Peter tells us that Jesus was bearing our sins on the tree, and Isaiah tells us that the Lord laid our iniquities on Him. This is the "Blanket of Filth." Two things were accomplished on "Groom Road." I learned that mankind was sick. The second lesson I learned was what Jesus did to make us well again. He endured the harsh, cruel words of men whom He created. He endured their hatred of pushing, shoving, spitting and slapping. He endured their beatings until He was bloody and marred passed recognition. After all the harsh treatment Jesus endured, He had the thick blanket of our perversions laid on Him.

After all the beatings and harsh words I endured, the last to come was an intimate violation. This was a deep offense, and my innocence was assaulted by this man's perversion touching my life. Each man's past, present and future acts of assaults, violations and offenses are one layer of perversion. Now, imagine layer after layer being lifted off the back of every man and laid on the back of one man until these layers upon layers become a thick "blanket of filth," thus making Himself the object of His Father's wrath against sin.

He took our place. Has anyone ever seen a Greater Love? I will end this chapter by telling you what the Lord spoke to me one day. I was getting dressed for work one morning. On my way out, I grabbed my coffee mug and headed for the front door. When I took hold of the door knob, the Lord stopped me with these words, "I do not give you what you want, I give you what I want. Man qualifies man in a class room, I qualify man by allowing him to be touched by it."

My precious friend, the next time you find yourself in the "house of affliction," know that you are on Groom Rd, and look forward to seeing what the Lord is qualifying you for.

Chapter Three

Whatever it Takes

𝕬 voice was heard in Ramah, lamentation
and bitter weeping, Rachel weeping for her
children, refusing to be comforted for her
children, because they are no more.
(Jer. 31:15)

B uckle in my precious friend, there is one more fiery
trial that we will look into; that you may see this
vessel being worked on, and what was wrought in my
life as a result. Then for the duration of this book, we will go
to the work shop that you may see how your Maker has been
having His way in your life. My Mother once told me,
"Wendy, you cannot always see God's hand in the fire, but
when you come through it, you can always look back and
see where His hand had been."

The title of this chapter "Whatever it Takes," was
actually a prayer of mine. This is quite the prayer, so pray it
only if you are prepared to trust God, to take you where that

might lead.

It seemed as though, with each stage of life, I was learning another aspect of Jesus. The Lord really wants us to know Him. It has been a great joy for me to share with you what the Lord has taught me. We have talked about the living waters of Christ, and just how very much alive He is. We have talked about the grooming of trials and understanding more of what Jesus has done for us. Now, I would like to share with you how Jesus does not loose what belongs to Him. We are not prone to losing what we have paid such a high price for.

After we were put in the street that late night by the "Preacher Man," our Mother drives us to Mississippi to live with our Dad, and then returned home. We did not know our Dad very well; but, I was looking forward to finding out who he was. I was excited to see his houseboat on the river. I had never seen a house floating on water before. He did appear to be a little unconventional in his ways. Seeing all of this, I thought, "no way, this is going to be awesome." Man, my Dad is cool! My brother and I had so much fun. We got to swim and fish. My Dad taught me how to catch crabs, so when I came home from school, I would run to the crab nets and pull them from the water to see if I got anything. We were able to run and play without fear. Boy what a feeling!

There did not appear to be very many rules. What kid does not find the happiness in this. However, I did notice in my new blissful life that we did not go to church anymore. Our new circle of family and friends never seem to mention the name of Jesus. So, there was no more Jesus. I missed hearing His name. There was no more music of worship and praise. There was no more playing my tambourine. In church we were accustomed to bright people clapping and dancing before the Lord; but, here I saw weary men fighting the battles of alcohol. In church we were used to the electrifying atmosphere of God's presence, but here the air was permeated with the dull aches of broken men. In church there was the tasting of our eternal joy's; but, here, there were only fleeting moments of worldly pleasures. I was learning what life without Jesus looked like, and it was terribly sad.

This new world I was living in had a certain fun to it, but it was dark. As a result, I suffered through more offenses. There were so many things I did not understand from my parent's point of view; but, from my view, no one that I knew could be trusted. Preachers were nothing more than wolves in sheep's clothing. Parents did not keep you safe; and, Jesus let it all happen. These brewing trains of thought formed the disastrous recipe that produced a stay in solitary confinement at the local jailhouse, and homes for troubled teens.

Tossed about in the waves of adversity, I would think about how I missed going to church and playing my tambourine. I would often think about the day Jesus and I laughed together and enjoyed each other's presence; but, I was hurt with Him because He put me in a world that had hurt me and made me feel unsafe at every turn. Nevertheless, as life's pains increased, I would close my eyes and look into the face of my Jesus, until I could see His living waters again. Remembering His words that my stay on earth would be temporary, helped me to take a deep breath and keep moving.

Not knowing when or if I would ever see Jesus again, I went on with my life and tried to put everything behind me in hopes to have a normal life. I'm not sure what "normal" truly means. Desperately trying to save what was left of my life, I became a mother of three and someone's wife by the time I was twenty-three years old. However, there is a scripture that warns those who seek to save their life (Matt. 10:39).

Believing in the reality of Jesus Christ was no hard thing for me, for how could I ever believe otherwise after what my eyes had seen, no matter what my experiences were? Yet I knew nothing about our day to day walk with Him. I was under the impression that we were just supposed to know that He was real, and if we could survive the hell on earth, then we got to go live with Him when it was over. Gee whiz, did I have a lot to learn.

I did not care much for the world I was put in; so, I created my own world. I opted for the "stay at home" mommy roll. Being a wife and mother was fulfilling in every way, and I seemed to have the perfect husband. He was handsome, successful and allowed me to stay at home with my children. To me, life could not be more perfect. My children and I were inseparable. I loved my children more than my life and would often make the comment that my children were my life.

After our time of playing together, I would tend to chores and make sure dinner was on the table. I would perform my religious duties by taking me and my children to church, and I would read my Bible when I had the time. I did not pray much though, but I knew Jesus understood my reasons for this. I had found the life I so longed for, and I was finally at peace. Everything was working as planned. This utopian world was a better place to live for me and my family. My surface life was a smoother way, with less pain. Therefore, it was easier to manage, so things did not get too painful for me again.

Yet, when I was alone, the Lord would gently deal with me in the deeper places. I was so glad to hear from Him because my soul ached for Him. I missed my Jesus very much, but I did not understand His ways. In my mind, He had made an awful world and I wanted out, but until then I had to find a way to be happy and at peace. I wanted no more turbulence and chaos. The life I made for myself was a place where I could survive, a place of safety from any more harm, besides I had finally found peace.

I did not realize that I was finding a life apart from the Lord, but He knew it. One evening while all were asleep, I slipped quietly into bed and propped my Bible on bended knees. I breathed out a gentle sigh over the unusually peaceful day I'd had. How nice it was I thought, to end my day with a relaxing read. Parting the pages of Scripture, my eyes fell straight to a certain section, and I was drawn to read. As I continued from verse to verse, my secure and happy world began to shake at the words of Jesus.

Think not that I am come to send peace on earth: I came not to send peace, but a sword. For I am come to set a man at variance against his father, and the daughter against her mother, and the

daughter-in-law against her mother-in-law,
and a man's foes shall be they of his
own household. He that loveth father
or mother more than me is not worthy
of me. And he that loveth son or daughter
more than me is not worthy of me. And
he that taketh not his cross, and
followeth after me, is not worthy of me.
He that findeth his life shall lose it,
and he that loseth his life for my sake
will find it. "
(Matt. 10:34-39)

My life changed right here...I knew, that I knew these words were for me. I thought about how I finally found some peace in my life, but if Jesus did not bring me the peace I was living in, then where did it come from, I wondered?

Peace I leave with you, My Peace I give
unto you; not as the world giveth, give
I unto you. Let not your heart be
troubled, neither let it be afraid.
(John 14:27)

My strong nature, short comings and radical beliefs in Jesus were quite the recipe for stirring up a few enemies within my family. However, when I reached the part about loving our son or daughter more than Jesus, and not being worthy of Him as a result. I knew I was in this category. Everyone that knew me knew my children came first in my life. When I read the part about, "He who finds his life will lose it," I knew beyond a shadow of a doubt, that I was about to experience the reality of this scripture. I could literally feel my olive skin turning pale, my heart bracing and sickness rising. I also knew that it would take a fight and a death, before I would let go of the peace and happiness I had found.

The blueness of a wound cleanseth away evil:
so, do stripes the inward parts of the belly.
(Prov. 20:30)

I knew with all my heart that I was about to endure a very difficult season. I did not know what it would be or when this would happen or any of the details, but I knew it was coming. All of a sudden, memories of meeting Jesus that day swept in on me like a mighty wind, and I was standing back in front of Jesus remembering my wild love and passion for Him. I realized that I had left my first love. I had forgotten what it felt like to really be alive.

To revisit His Living Waters again brought the hard truth of my thirsty and malnourished condition. To be reminded of the real Love, the real Joy and the real Peace that is in Jesus crashed my utopian world of false peace. Every memory rushed to the forefront presenting evidence of my error. At this moment, I realized that I had been gently deceived with the subtleties of false peace. It is impossible to leave the source of life and still expect to live.

Jesus loves us in a wild way; so, we must believe Him when He says He is jealous over us (Exod. 20:5). His presence is a perpetual pouring forth of the knowledge of His existence. To be in the presence of The Eternal Lover is to be saturated in Love. His Love has the beautiful power to bring the soul to a sweet place of surrender, as it graciously overwhelms and conquers everything in you. Oh, to be baptized in the love of Jesus Christ.

It's a strange thing to say, but somehow, I knew Jesus was coming for me after all these years. It was time to come home. I did not know how to get back to Him; so, I surrendered with this prayer: "Lord, whatever I have to go through down here, so that when I stand before You one day, my ears will hear, "Well done thy good and faithful servant," then let it be done unto me; because, "Depart from me, I never knew you," is not an option for me. So, whatever it takes Lord; whatever it takes."

Within 6 months, my home, car, finances, material possessions, my husband, and all of my children were removed from my life. Not through physical death, but very much gone. My wages were garnished for child support; so, I paid child support for several years. The battle finally wore me down until I could not function and hold a job. I was so broken. Not being able to make my payments, I was arrested and jailed twice. During this time, I stayed fighting for my children in the same courtroom for ten years; but, all to no avail.

My face was to the ground with the worst pain I had ever known; and, it stayed this way for seventeen-years. The pain was unspeakable. My appetite left, much of my hair fell out; and, I became weak through weight loss. I fought through various illnesses, and my years of grieving left me with internal bleeding. My body was racked with pain which could not be medically explained. Trying to maintain a morsel of sanity, as I made my way through college, was challenging. My thoughts were so dominated by this tragedy, until I found myself head on with an eighteen-wheeler, and his horn was the only thing that spared us both. I left off driving for a season.

Every aspect of my life was being affected. Nothing was left untouched even to the point of losing my eyesight one day. I just went totally blind. Each day seemed to be a new challenge. Nearing the end of the seventeenth-year stretch, boils began to break out on me, starting with my face. The humiliation was inconceivable. The boils that I could tend to I would. The ones I could not reach, I had surgically removed. The boils were painful and lasted for a period of five months. Doctors were doing everything they could to help me, but I had something to go through that man could make no pill for.

Throughout this time of affliction, the Lord would do things from time to time to reach out to me, but I was not willing. I am most ashamed to say this now, but no one could even mention the Lord's name around me, before the bitterness of my soul would rise. Many caring friends would try to encourage me throughout the years, but I refused comfort of any kind. The loss of my children was, to me, the loss of my own soul. I was another Rachel.

*A voice was heard in Ramah, lamentation
and bitter weeping, Rachel weeping for her
children, refusing to be comforted for her
children, because they are no more.*
(Jer. 31:15)

I clung to Job's story in the scriptures. Desperate to learn how he was able to hold his integrity as he bared the pains of his greatest loss. I could clearly see that Job's trial was on a greater scale than mine; and, yet, his attitude surpassed mine in every way. The only book I would read for nearly a year was the book of Job, and yet it seemed to be getting darker for me. I was really losing hope for the first time in my life. Behind the wheel of my car, I began to pray. In my anguish I told the Lord that either He could take me out of this world, or I would do it. Either way, I could not bear it anymore. I reached a scary place of peace knowing I meant every word of it. Right in the middle of my hopeless state, the Lord speaks, "How will you know who I am, unless you've walked the ways that I have walked?"

*That I may know Him, and the power of
His resurrection, and the fellowship of His
sufferings, being made conformable unto
His death.*
(Phil. 3:10)

I immediately remembered what Job told his wife when she said, "Curse God and die." He said, "Should we only accept the good and not the bad?" I began to cry and weep before my Lord with repentance, knowing I was only willing to have the good and not the bad.

Then said his wife unto him, Dost thou still
retain thine integrity? Curse God and die.
but he said unto her, Thou speakest as one
of the foolish women speaketh. What? Shall
we receive good at the hand of God, and shall
we not receive evil? In all this did not Job sin
with his lips.
(Job 2:9-10)

Jesus was relentless in His pursuits and refused to give up on me. Still, refusing comfort of any kind, the Lord arranged something miraculous; using time, places and people to bring me a powerful truth. One that would forever change my limited view of God and how He operates in our lives. Recalling the account, I received an invitation to fly to Jerusalem, Israel, for a visit with my brother who was in pursuit of his biblical studies. I stayed with a pastor and his family, along with my brother. They were very gracious to me and allowed me to stay during my visit.

The pastor's wife was a strong woman, whom I felt drawn to. Knowing my story, she knocked on the door of my greatest wound, "Wendy, your brother told me that you lost your children." I braced as the winds of mixed emotions blew through me like a hurricane. I thought, "What words could ever be used to redeem a soul that's past the point of no return?" Nevertheless, I continued to listen in hopes that somehow her words would pull me back to the side of hope. She continues to tell me of a mother who had five children, and how she brought them to the babysitter on her way to work one day. When she returned for them, she discovered that her ex-husband had kidnapped all her children, and she did not see them again until twenty-five years later. The pastor's wife also related to me that a movie had been made based on their life story, and that at the end they would show the real Mother and all five of her children together again.

This dear lady had my attention, and I found myself later that evening watching their story. Of course, the movie was just as she had told me, and I saw the now aged mother sitting with her children at the end. I, too, had to wonder, "Lord will my head turn gray, as well, before I see my children?" I was grateful for her courage to reach out to me, and I was also glad to see all five of these children reunited with their mother. However, I was so buried in a prison of pain and hardness until the only thing I had the ability to feel anymore was the dead numbness of being over-medicated.

Waking up the next morning, I could feel a deep stirring as if something good was about to happen. I had not felt anything like that in years. This strengthened me enough to get up and go to church with the pastor and his family. I knew the preaching of Jesus Christ in Jerusalem was not something I wanted to miss. I just assumed this was why I was feeling so good, but there was more to it.

When the service ended, the pastor's wife came over and took me by the hand. She explained there was someone she wanted me to meet. Walking me to the other side of the room, we stop in front of a 5' 7", mid-forties man, with dark hair and a beard. The pastor's wife introduces me in a way I was not expecting, "Wendy, I would like for you to meet the real son of the mother you saw in the movie last night. This is one of her sons that was taken from her for twenty-five years." The impact of her words hit me so hard until it blew apart all that I had been shielding myself with and left me utterly speechless. As I stood looking at the son of this hero of a mother, I began weeping until I lost control, and my broken mess of a life was on display in front of a perfect stranger. I had no time to concern myself with humiliation, I had to have some answers.

This brother in the Lord begins, "Ma'am, I see the pain you are in. May I pray for you?" I nodded, and he took the oil, touched my forehead and began praying. After a few minutes, he just stopped in midstream, and said, "Wendy, do you remember the prayer that you prayed all those years ago?" I lifted my head, as I wondered what prayer he could be referring to. Furthermore, I thought "What man could know the prayers of another?" Nevertheless, I braced myself for his words. He said, "You have asked God to do whatever it takes, that when you stand before Him one day, you will hear "Well done, thy good and faithful servant." He wants you to know that He has only answered what you prayed. This was His answer, and this is what it took."

At this truth, I was released from my prison of anguish, and my knees fell to a place of surrender. My face landed upon the breast of my first love as I breathed in His

Faithfulness. To know that He actually heard my prayer, astounded me. To see the distance He would go to answer my prayer made me a believer. To know that He was preparing my ears to hear the words, "Well Done," revealed my eternal destination. Oh, my soul is not lost. Jesus has come for me! To see a Love that refused to quit spoke of a Love that could outlast a defiant heart screaming in pain. To see a Love that was unrelenting, unmovable, unshakeable, and eternally faithful by nature was to see the place of my refuge. I thought my reckless activities and furious pursuits to annihilate the pain had brought my soul to the land of no redemption. I thought I was suffering in ways that somehow He did not know about. However, in that moment, I realized that pain did not have the power to carry me to a place that Jesus could not find me.

He knew exactly what He was doing, and the perfect time to turn the fires down. For He truly is the one who created the smith to blow on the coals in the fire until He is satisfied we have become a worthy instrument (Isa.54:16). I have well discovered that if God said it, He means it. God will have no one come before Him. He is a jealous God, just as we are told. Believe Him (Exod. 34:14)!

Idolatry in the heart is no light matter and will require an anvil, the circumcision made without hands, and a Love that will hold you there until the work is finished (Col. 2:11). I was not the same after that day, and it changed me in a radical way, to know how serious God is about His word. He operates in a Truth that the carnal mind cannot endure (2 Tim. 4:3). God in no way thinks like us (Isa.55:8-9).

Seeing Jesus in the lowest place I had ever known, convinced me that we could go nowhere without His knowledge of it (Ps. 139). For years, I wandered around as though I had lost my own soul, but Jesus does not lose what His Father has given to Him (John 17:12). Our time of trials are never wasted; and, much work is being accomplished; that we may stand before our eternal Father unashamed and without spot or wrinkle (Eph.5:27). So, let us take courage and thank the Lord for loving us enough to finish the work He has started (Phil. 1:6).

As a little girl, Jesus introduced Himself as the One who loved me first. As the One who had Love, Joy and Peace. He introduced Himself as The Way, The Truth and The Life, and as the Fountain of Living Waters. It was not until I was broken and brought past my ability to recover, that He found me years later and introduced Himself as my Redeemer. I went to Jerusalem a smoking flax, but, I returned home a blazing fire (Isa. 32:3). Instead of my despairing walk among the tombstones, I could feel life again. Oh, how much easier it is to breathe when hope is in the air. I was reminded all over again that I could see Him in everything and in any circumstance. I just had to be willing to see Him.

This set the fire to me in a real way, and I returned to the States and back to my office. I leaned over my desk, stretched out my drawings of piped vessel's, and instead of seeing the operations of the industry, I could see me and you in operation. I ran to the shop to the place where I stood so many times before; but, this time, as I watched the sharp object lower and sever the unwanted portion, I could see the blade of circumcision lay into the heart of every believer.

Hearing the grinding noises on another vessel caught my attention, and I could see the ponderings of a weary deliverer, as Moses wandered through unknown territory in preparation to stand in front of Egypt's ruler. Hearing the forklift, I turned to see Esther being carried to the palace for the preparation to stand against the annihilation of her people. The striking sounds in another area had me curious, and I could see Elijah pounded into shape until he was able to confront the lying prophets of Jezebel. As the fired torch laid into another vessel, I could see the hot coal purging the lips of Isaiah. Leaving the shop, I could see a stainless-steel vessel waiting for its inspection. As I ran my hand across this mighty piece of steel, I thought about the brazen walls of Jeremiah. Returning to my office, I looked over as a massive vessel was undergoing the pressures of a heavy testing, and I could hear the speech of integrity, as Job proclaimed, "Though He slay me, yet will I trust Him.

Which gladly brings me to the purpose of this book. I believe the Lord would have you know how much He loves you, and that He really does know what He is doing with us. We are truly in the palm of His hand. Our pains have purpose. The Lord is purging us, building us and getting us ready. So, we need a little time in the shop.

I pray that as you continue through this book, you will be able to see yourself being worked on in the shop and come to know that God has a real purpose in all you are being made to endure. Your time of preparation is making you ready to work in the field. Let the Lord have His way because our time is short; the harvest is plentiful; and, laborers are needed. Now, put on your safety glasses my precious one, and let's go to shop and watch our Father work.

But now, O Lord, thou art our father;
we are the clay, and thou our potter;
and we all are the work of thy hand.
(Isaiah 64:8)

Chapter Four

The Plan

❧❦❧

For I know the thoughts that I think toward you, saith the Lord, thoughts of peace, and not of evil, to give you an expected end. (Jer. 29:11)

According to Merriam-Webster, "design means to create, fashion, execute or construct according to plan." Other descriptions are, to devise for a specific function, to have a purpose for, or to conceive and plan out in the mind. Let's take a synoptic view, regarding a designer of pipe. This entails going to the drawing board, rolling out the past and present plans for a review, knowing there is a need for change in the field.

Once completed, the next phase is to send a field engineer to the site to see where the placement of the design will be. The existing drawing will serve as a point of reference. However, live measurements are needed, as well as an overview for various obstacles that might hinder the design. Taking all into account, the field engineer draws a preliminary sketch, or outline, to show the main components of what is to be executed. According to Genesis 1:1, In the beginning God created the heavens and the earth. From the beginning, God had us know Him as the Designer and creator of all things.

During my time in the Piping Industry, I had the opportunity to accompany a field engineer. I saw vessels of pipe everywhere and in every direction working as a team, functioning in their particular purpose. Seeing this, was a reminder of a parable Jesus taught concerning a field. When the disciples asked Him to explain its meaning, Jesus says, "He that soweth the good seed is the Son of man; The field is the world; the good seeds are the children of the kingdom; but the tares are the children of the wicked one (Matt.13:37-38)."

We see that God is "The Designer" who has created this field. His son, Jesus Christ is the sower. The good seeds are us who belong to His kingdom, and He has planted us in the field for a purpose. I have been gleaning through the Scriptures for most of my life and I have yet to find where God ever made a move without purpose. Therefore, do not despair. Your life, your struggles are not without purpose. Now, if you have not already, this is a good place to shout. As a matter of fact, why don't you take a short break, lay this book down, and give the Lord a shout of praise, and add a good old fashion Hallelujah dance! It will put a smile on His face. Believe me!

When the idea has been conceived in the mind of the designer, he sets out to build a model of his intention through drawings. Drawings are the laid-out plan, full of various components; including but not limited to, pipe configurations, their attachments, symbolic notations, mathematics, orientation, etc. The plan shows a view from nearly every angle; so, there is no doubt as to what the designer requires for the making of all the vessels. His plan includes many vessels, as well as a wealth of knowledge and information as to how to handle each one.

The designer demonstrates in picture form the various attachments each vessel is to have for production. If the vessel is to have a support system attached to it, this will be indicated on the drawing as well. An emblem of the north, south, east and west arrow is usually stamped in the upper left-hand corner of the drawing, indicating the vessel's orientation and direction it will go. The plan also displays the various vessels working as a team once they have been placed in the field for operation. There is a component welded to each end of the pipe vessel, known as the "flange." This is a round steel plate, with bolt holes. When the vessels reach the field, their flanges are brought together and bolted tight, joining the two. When another vessel arrives in the field, its flange is joined to another flanged piece already in operation. So, the body of vessels enlarge and work together as a team, according to plan.

Another pocket of information can be found within the various forms of mathematics. The math tells us the size of all the vessels. Another form of math may indicate a ¼" slope on the team of vessels, which tells me that one end of the working team will be higher than the other end, thus causing the service to flow through each vessel. A vessel needs to be elevated on one end to pour into another vessel. The math that indicates the elevation, reveals whether that vessel is to take a low position or a high position, once it reaches the field and is set in place for operation.

As we already know, not all of us are called to pastor a church; but, we, as sheep, are various members of one body. We are connected to the head and function where we have been placed, as the Designer has ordained.

The pipe designer's plan will also give a list of materials which indicates the various attachments the vessels will have welded to it to feed other vessels and work as one. So, the plan or drawings are my instructions in picture form.

The set of specifications that come with the drawings are my instructions in written form. The pictures are reminiscent of how the Lord allows us to have visions and dreams. Our written instructions, of course, are the Scriptures. God knows the plan He has for each vessel of His, and how we are to function and work together as a team to do His will.

For I know the thoughts that I think toward
you, says the Lord, thoughts of peace, and
not of evil, to give you an expected end.
(Jer. 29:11)

Specifications are a set of documented requirements, usually of a technical nature, provided by the designer/engineer. Also referred to as a "set of specs." Each specification could be seen as a small book revealing in detail what is required for that particular portion of the job. For example, carbon steel would not have the same requirements that the Stainless-Steel metal has. They are different and have their own purpose. There is a detailed set of instructions for each metal.

A careful study shows what kind of metal is to be used along with its grade or (quality). The specification will also indicate its schedule or wall thickness as well as its various attachments, supports, etc. Any deviation from these written laws could prove to be disastrous. Concerning the "Walls of a Metal," I am reminded of what God said to His Prophet. In Jeremiah 1:18, God tells Jeremiah that He made him a defenced city, an iron pillar and brazen walls, against the whole land. Jeremiah had some thick walls (skin). He was made very strong. Yet, again, just a few chapters over we read in Jeremiah 15:20, that God made him a "Fenced Brazen Wall," because the people would fight against him. Our Designer knew how to build His Prophet.

In the piping industry, those working with the vessel make absolutely no decisions as to what the vessel itself will become. This has already been established by the Designer. We pipe drafters, pipe fitters, welders and so on, are only allowed to be a part of the plan by adhering to the guide lines set forth by the Designer. The written requirements also give a detailed list as to what the vessel will endure before reaching its destination. In other words, how much pressure the vessel can take before breaking. One requirement would be the vessel's time of testing. The specifications would also give instructions as to what methods would be used for the testing of the work performed, and of the metal itself. From beginning to end, the Manual has covered all bases pertaining to the vessel for the duration of its existence in the field. Without the "Set of Specs," it would be impossible to know in detail what is required for the vessel or what would be required of those who would be working with the vessel, for that matter. It is important to note that when the vessels are delivered, so are their manuals.

As we all know, manuals are truly in place for a reason. Without instructions we are left to our own understanding. To illustrate this, let us envision my cousin Boudreaux knocking on my door with all smiles with a bicycle in hand. Professing that he has assembled it just for me, while simultaneously boasting of how he required no instruction. In his way of thinking the manual was simply of no use to him, because his knowledge was all that was needed! Are we able to get a glimpse of what's coming down the pike here, in this scenario?

I can nearly imagine going downhill on a beautiful country road, as my white linen dress taps gently against my ankles. The wind lifting my hair in its summer breeze, as I breathe in a fresh sense of freedom. The scenery is majestic. The dense green trees, and tall swaying flowers touches my eyes with delight. The over lapping trees provide just enough shade to shield me from the heat. Lifting my hand for a happy wave to an elderly neighbor tending his garden, I hear a clunk of metal hit the pavement, sending sparks of fire up towards my feet. Trying desperately to maintain control, the handle bars make a shift in a downward motion, throwing my upper torso on top of the bike. Now that my life is in total jeopardy and I am gasping for my last breath on this side of heaven, the handle bars rattle loose and land in a nearby field. All because Boudreaux couldn't see the need for that screw. Now that the bike is picking up speed, and I am trying to hold tight to what is left of the handle bars, the front wheel decides to do a shimmy and a shake, until it flies right into a windshield of a ninety-two-year-old woman coming home from a bake sale. An innocent lady, a mother, a dedicated volunteer, and a loving grandmother strapped to a bed, for the remainder of her days, and I am in the next room on life support.

But you see Boudreaux had it all under control; and assured me that he had no need for the instructions, because he was smart enough to figure this thing out on his own. We need the Manual, brothers and sisters. We need the Manual. God is the Designer, Engineer and Creator of all that we can see and of all that we cannot see. His manual of requirements (The Bible) has great purpose and is very much necessary. Deviation from our Creator's manual has proven to be unwise and devastatingly costly to say the least.

The "Set of Specs," in the engineers' manual reminds me of the "Set of Books" in the Bible. Each book is important and has been strategically placed in the whole of God's Manual for a real purpose. The Manual (Bible) is the written Word revealing the plan we are to follow in life. God's manual covers every aspect of our lives and for the duration thereof. For every change or circumstance we would endure, God already provided all the instructions. The Bible is like no other book in the entirety of the world.

The words written in the Bible are "Alive" and have "Life" in them.

It is the spirit that quickeneth; the flesh profiteth nothing: the words that I speak unto you, they are spirit, and they are life. (John 6:63)

God's Word is the "Bread" you eat for your spirit to have the nourishment it needs to live. When we spend time in the Word, we are feeding on the "Bread of Life." Jesus tells us that He is this Bread (John 6:32-35). It brings great joy to my heart to know that when this vessel came to earth, I was given my set of instructions (Bible), that I may know the way I should go and where my place is in the field. All scripture is given by inspiration of God and is profitable for doctrine, for reproof, for correction, for instruction in righteousness (2 Tim.3:16). I am also filled with tremendous comfort to know that God's Word will still be standing when all else has come to its end.

The grass withereth, the flower fadeth: but The word of our God shall stand forever. (Isa. 40:8)

Heaven and earth shall pass away: but My words shall not pass away. (Luke 21:33)

Being born again, not of corruptible seed, but of incorruptible, by the word of God, which liveth and abideth forever. For all flesh is as grass, and all the glory of man as the flower of grass. The grass withereth, and the flower thereof falleth away: But the word of the Lord endureth forever. And this is the word which by the gospel is preached unto you (1Pet. 1:23-25)

Chapter Five

Working with the Vessel

**J will praise thee; for J am fearfully
and wonderfully made: marvelous
are thy works; and that my soul
knoweth right well.
(Ps.139:14)**

Now that the designer has devised a strategy, it is time to set all things in motion by choosing the vessel that will fit his plan. He knows that he needs a vessel that can house something powerful because it will serve a specific purpose of fueling other vessels. As well as, helping to maintain the necessary level of activity in the field.

The vessel will have a most important task. Therefore, a large investment of work will be allocated to this vessel. Knowing the plan, the engineer will list out all that is required. He starts by deciding what material the vessel will need to be. There are various materials to choose from: Carbon, Stainless, Titanium, Monel and so forth. The metal will need to be of a high quality, have durability, strength and a resistance to corrosion. A commonly used metal with these attributes is the Stainless-Steel metal. The Scriptures reveal a list of materials used for vessels as well.

> *But in a great house there are not only*
> *vessels of gold and silver, but also of*
> *wood and clay, some for honor and some*
> *for dishonor. Therefore, if anyone cleanses*
> *himself from the latter, he will be a vessel*
> *for honor, sanctified and useful for the Master,*
> *prepared for every good work.*
> *(2 Tim. 2:20-21)*

Looking at our brother, Paul, for a moment, we discover where Jesus entered his life and forever changed him. The Lord reveals to us that Paul is His chosen vessel (Acts 9:15-16). He then lets us know what He will use him for, and the hardships that will be his companion. Jeremiah was another chosen vessel by God for a specific work, which is found in (Jer.1:5). Little David was also chosen of God and taken from the sheepfolds to be a King (Ps 78:70).

The next Scripture I would like to mention should bring every child of God great comfort in knowing that we ourselves are chosen. The scripture reads, "If the world hate you, ye know that it hated me before it hated you. If ye were of the world, the world would love its own: but because ye are not of the world, but I have chosen you out of the world, therefore the world hateth you (John 15:18-19). No matter the various troubles we endure, there is a great comfort in knowing that we were chosen by God Himself.

In 2 Timothy 2:4 we read, "No man who wars entangles himself with the affairs of this life; that he may please Him Who has chosen him to be a soldier." So, here we can see that we are chosen to be soldiers. A soldier is to stay focused on the task at hand, and not be side tracked with the cares of this world. We do not live to please men, but God and Him alone. There is much work to be done in the making of a soldier. Let's take a small rabbit trail and peek into a man's life who was learning about this war we find ourselves in. The prophet, Jeremiah, was truly in the heat of the battle, and he was becoming weary. He was hated by nearly all who knew him, to the point that his enemies sought to take his life.

In Jeremiah 12:1-5, we read a dialog between the exhausted prophet and His Maker. Jeremiah questions why the wicked prosper, and how it is that treacherous people can live happy lives. His frustration continues until he settles down for the Lord's answer. Now, God responds to Jeremiah with this question, "If thou hast run with the footmen, and they have wearied thee, then how canst thou contend with horses? And if in the land of peace, wherein thou trustedst, they wearied thee, then how wilt thou do in the swelling of

Jordan?" After this, the Lord encouraged Jeremiah, because He knew that Jeremiah had greater battles ahead, and by chapter thirteen, we see Jeremiah getting up and going back to work. Our brother was becoming quite the soldier. Just as God encouraged and strengthened this chosen vessel, He will do the same for us. We have been weary in the battle, but God is working on us because a greater battle lies ahead. Revelation 17:14 reads this way, "These shall make war with the Lamb, and the Lamb shall overcome them; for He is Lord of lords, and King of kings: and they who are with Him are called, and chosen, and faithful."

Here we see that chosen vessels will stand with the King of kings at this great battle, where we will partake in the defeat of our enemy. We are being prepared for a great battle that will end with a mighty sweet victory my friend. Let God arise, let his enemies be scattered: let them also that hate him flee before him. As smoke is driven away, so drive them away: as wax melteth before the fire, so let the wicked perish at the presence of God (Ps. 68:1).

In the piping industry, once the vessel has been chosen, it is brought straight to the cutting machine. A sharp blade will be lowered to cut the pipe to the length specified on the drawing, "Ouch!" After the vessel has been cut, it is brought to the next setup station, and propped on a set of jack stands. A couple of men known as the "Fitters," balance and fit the vessel with its various components; according to what the drawing plan has indicated, such as; elbows, tees, reducers, flanges and so forth. At this point another set of men known as the "Tackers," step up and make three small tack welds around each joint. This will hold the joint in place for the Welder. The welder then gets ready to do his part. The vessel will endure a season of heat and pressure, as the welder merges all the working parts into one body. A common method of welding is called, "stick welding." This method requires a narrow stick of metal that matches the metal he is working on. With tools and gear, he flips his hood over his face, bears down on the vessel with a torch in one hand, the stick of metal in the other. He fires the stick in the groove of the joint, and melts both metals until they liquify into a puddle, and like the hands of an artist the welder moves the stick back and forth causing the liquid metals to merge until the fitting has become one with the body.

Every joint on this vessel will be welded from the inside out. The welder makes three passes around each joint, and each pass has its own name. The first pass is called the "root pass." This pass welds the inside diameters of the two pieces together. The second pass is called the "intermediate pass." This welds the midsection. The third pass is called the "cover pass." This welds the outside together. The vessel experiences fire with each pass. After the main body of the vessel has become a whole piece with its additions, the next phase, if required, will be the adding of various branches and supports. This, of course, will cause the vessel to endure more sharp cuts, heat, fire and pressure. There is a scripture that reminds me of a sharp cut to the heart. But he is a Jew, which is one inwardly; and Circumcision is that of the heart, in the spirit, and not in the letter; whose praise is not of men, but of God (Rom. 2:9).

Just like the piped vessel that endures the cuttings, the fired torches, and various pressures, so also it is the same with us, when the Lord is having His way. All of this is for a real purpose. Without this necessary work, the vessel would remain a single pipe that could do nothing but lay there and be useless. There would be no need to run anything through a single piece of pipe. It would just go in one end and out the other. There is nothing to hold or contain the service. Without the attachment of the elbow fitting, how would the service running through turn in any certain direction? Without the flange being welded to the end of the pipe, how would the piece hook to another vessel in the field, so the service can run from vessel to vessel? Without the smaller attachments, how could the vessel feed the others they come in contact with?

Our times of tribulations are truly not in vain, but are working in us the necessary attributes that we will need for our work in the field. For in the Scriptures we read, "And not only so, but we glory in tribulations also: knowing that tribulation worketh patience; and patience, experience; and experience, hope" (Rom. 5:3-4). Be encouraged, my dear friend, and know that the Designer knew from the beginning what it would take for you to become useful for a work.

The Branches

The vessel by now has been remarkably transformed and is really something to see, it is larger and stronger than when it first entered the shop. With all the work, along with its new counter parts. The main vessel is referred to as the "header." The vessel will have to be very strong and powerful because it will have other vessels pulling from it once it goes to the field. As a result, it will endure a longer stay in the fabrication shop because more work is required.

The Header piece will forgo a series of cuts for the addition of various attachments; commonly referred to as the "branches". Looking at the definition of a branch we find that it is something that extends from or enters a main body or source. A branch is also referred to as an extension of activities.

When my mind would become weary with mulling over pipe configurations and mathematical formulas, I would grab a cup of coffee and make my way to the shop to watch someone else work for a while. It was always neat to watch the vessel's process. As I lifted my cup for a drink, I watched a worker of steel lower his hood, raise his tool, and carve out an open area in the header piece or main body. I understood he was making a way for the grafting of a branch. Once he adjusted the branch to a suitable fit, he wrapped his hand around a torch like tool, fired it up and melted the two metals until they were joined. As I watched this process, a deep satisfaction rolled over me as I began recalling my studies in the Scriptures pertaining to grafted branches (Rom. 11:16-24). Nothing excites me more than to see God's word in action.

Once the branch has been grafted into the Header, it now has access to what is flowing through the main body. At field installation, smaller vessels will be attached to the branches of the main body. The Header will then supply the branches with what they need for operation, and the branches will supply the ones they come in contact with. However, due to the massive size of this vessel, and what will be required of it, the vessel will need support once it reaches the field. So, looking to the designer's plan, a detailed view of the support is drawn out, along with the list of materials needed to build the support itself, as well as instructions regarding the supports position. We may not always like who God chooses to put with us in the field as our support, but God knows what that vessel is capable of.

Nevertheless, since our story has to do with a designer, a header and a branch, let's look at what the apostle John recorded.

> *I am the True Vine, and My Father is the*
> *Husbandman. Every branch in Me that bears*
> *not fruit He takes away: and every branch that*
> *bears fruit, He purges it, that it may bring forth*
> *more fruit. Now you are clean through the Word*
> *which I have spoken unto you. Abide in me,*
> *and I in you. As the branch cannot bear fruit*
> *of itself, except it abide in the Vine; no more*
> *can you, except you abide in Me. I am the Vine,*
> *you are the branches: he who abides in Me,*
> *and I in him, the same brings forth much fruit:*
> *for without Me you can do nothing.*
> *If a man abide not in Me, he is cast forth*
> *as a branch and is withered; and men gather*
> *them, and cast them into the fire, and they*
> *are burned. If you abide in Me and My Words*
> *abide in you, you shall ask what you will,*
> *and it shall be done unto you (John 15:1-7).*

So, here we see that the Husbandman or (Designer) is God the Father. The True Vine or (Header) is Jesus. The branch is us. Jesus has told us that He is the Way, the Truth and the Life (John 14:6). If we as branches are not grafted into "The Way," then we have chosen another way to walk, which always leads us in the wrong direction. If not grafted into "The Truth," then what is there left to believe in but lies. If not grafted into "The Life," then we die.

Who approaches a child to do them harm while their Father is standing next to them? It is very important that we stay connected to The Way, so we are not led into a different way, separating us from our Father. We need to stay connected to The Truth, so we will not be snared by the traditions of men and their philosophies. We need to stay connected to The Life that we may continue to live and not be lost for all of eternity.

Check

As a young girl, I had an encounter with a Man that changed my life. His name is Jesus. I have been amazed by Him ever since. The more I learn about Him, the more amazed I become. The way Jesus uses parables to teach spiritual truths is one of the things He does that just absolutely astounds me. I find it incredible that He could reveal an invisible reality, by using what could be seen and understood by man, while at the same time bringing deep truths to a heart and mind that is void of understanding and real knowledge.

Just as Jesus used a sheep herder, a farmer of land, and one who tends a vineyard as examples to reveal a truth, so also, He will use our way of living to personally teach us a truth. Jesus said, "I am the Truth." He wants us to know Him. In Biblical times, Jesus used their everyday workings to teach them. He has not changed. If we will look for Jesus in our everyday activities, we will see Him because He is everywhere. He really does want us to know Him. When you really see how this works, your life will be so filled with Joy until it will be all you can do not to act like a complete idiot at times. I tell you, when I realized that I could see Jesus everywhere and in everything, well… I have not been the same since. Please believe me when I say, you can go nowhere that Jesus is not already there. Our eyes must learn how to see Him. Spending time in His Word will be a good place to start.

Learning about the "check valve" in the piping industry was interesting. I was intrigued by its function, its purpose and even its name, "check." The check valve is something that is welded into the line or built into the vessel as a check mechanism. If the flow of service running through the piped vessel backs up and tries to go in the wrong direction, a flap in the check valve drops in place to block the service from going the wrong way.

After working with check valves for several years, I finally noticed some characteristics I had not seen previously. I realized that we have various check mechanisms the Lord has built into our lives. Our conscience is one of these mechanisms that really bothers us when we are taking off in a wrong direction. It is the mechanism that causes us to perceive or apprehend a thing, or to notice something with a degree of controlled thought or observation. Intuition is another one that sends a signal that something is off, whether we can put our finger on it or not. It is to contemplate a matter or to have quick and ready insight.

We get what we call a "gut feeling" when something is not right. Christians who are familiar with the Spirit-filled life have a more power packed mechanism. When we are about to make a wrong decision that will lead us in a wrong direction, the Holy Spirit will nudge us with a little Check in our spirit as a warning signal to block or hinder a wrong way. The Holy Spirit is the One Who leads us into all truth, thus keeping us in the right direction. Howbeit when he, the Spirit of Truth, is come, he will guide you into all truth: for he shall not speak of himself; but whatsoever he shall hear, that shall he speak: and he will shew you things to come (John 16:13).

Wisdom, Knowledge and Discernment are powerfully enhanced mechanisms built into the life of the believer to stop the flow of a wrong direction. These are wonderful attributes, gifts and privileges that belong to God's children. I will praise thee; for I am fearfully and wonderfully made: marvelous are thy works; and that my soul knoweth right well (Ps.139:14).

Check-Out Time

Now that the vessel has finally been processed through the shop with all its additions, it is time to go to the check-out counter. This is where a worker in the trade will examine the fabricated work along with the drawing plan side by side. He checks everything. He looks at the vessel from every angle. He checks to make sure the vessel is the right size. He makes sure the vessel's metal is consistent with the plan. He checks its wall thickness (skin). He examines the vessel's orientation (direction). The checker also scans the list of material to see if the vessel has all its working parts along with the proper support that might be needed - once it reaches the field. He makes sure that it has everything the Designer said it should have.

The check-out person must pay attention and have a good eye for detail because he is the last person to see this portion of the work. If something does not sit right with the check-out guy, then he will stop the entire process. He will pull everyone who worked on the vessel, if need be, until he is satisfied the vessel is fully equipped with everything it will need to function properly. On the other hand, if the checker's requirements are satisfied, the vessel will be released for the next phase, which usually means a testing of some sort.

Chapter Six

The Furnace

Behold I have refined you,
but not with silver;
I have chosen you in the
furnace of affliction.
(Isa.48:10)

As I watched all that a vessel had to endure in the shop, I knew from experience that there was more to come. There were contaminates within the vessel that needed to be addressed, along with certain procedures and various testings of the metal before it was field worthy. There is a procedure (or fiery trial) called "Stress Relieving". This requirement is determined by the Designer/Engineer when it is necessary. The Stress Relieving process benefits the vessel in multiple ways. One purpose is to relieve the vessel of stress, hence the name; another is to purify the vessel by ridding the metal of all contaminants, among other things which we will see.

If the Designer/Engineer decides that the vessel will carry a non-explosive service such as water, then a lower grade metal like Carbon Steel would suffice and would not require various procedures and strenuous testing. On the other hand, if the vessel is to house something powerful and explosive, then a higher grade of metal would be required. Therefore, the vessel must endure what is necessary according to how it will be used. The vessel must be trust worthy if it has the potential to harm, due to its explosive service.

Stress Relieving is the process of heating materials to a suitable temperature and holding that temperature long enough to reduce stress, or internal stress, that remains after the original cause of stress has been removed. This is followed by the process of cooling the material slowly to minimize the development of new residential stress. Stress Relieving is not intended to change the micro-structure or mechanical properties significantly, it is purely intended to allow the steel to remain "Stress-Free" during the manufacturing process and throughout its life cycle.

Have you ever been through a very painful trial that brought a tremendous amount of stress in your life? Did the pain become so intense that you could feel yourself turning hard? Our painful trials produce certain stresses that cannot be seen which are the internal stresses. We can talk to a close friend or a family member in hopes to alleviate some external or surface stress, but it takes a fiery heat to reach our internal stresses because we have become hard. Let's look at some more reasons why we might be enduring a season in the furnace.

The common name in the piping industry for stress relieving a vessel is called PWHT (Post Weld Heat Treat). Meaning: After the vessel has been welded, it will endure a treatment of heat. Heat treating a vessel is for the purpose of improving the characteristics of the metal or bringing its character back to a desirable standard which may have been affected during the transformation process. During welding, the vessel has become inflamed due to the intense heat, thus causing the metal to transform through various metallurgical phases. Depending on the chemistry of the metals in the area being treated, a hardening begins to occur. Hardness in the metal has taken place because it was at its highest point of stress. Because the vessel has been maxed out in the stress arena, a "Stress Relieving" procedure is necessary.

So, at the highest points of our heat, pain and stress, our hearts take on a hardness which cannot be helped. The hardness has occurred for good reason; we are being worked on to merge our metal with the various things God desires to make apart of us. It takes heat to join something to a metal.

The Heat Treatment procedure is designed to alleviate the stress by reducing the hardness and increasing ductility, thus reducing the danger of cracking. Let's peel this wordy statement back a bit, that we may see the richness of what is really taking place here. We see three things occurring in the vessel while it's made to endure this heat. There is a reducing of hardness, an increase in ductility and a reduction in the danger, or possibilities of the vessel cracking. Again, the hardness we feel is due to the stresses we have been under. So, God in His wisdom knows it's time for the heat, so we will become soft again. Job talked about God making his heart soft (Job 23:16). Increasing Ductility is a fitting phrase. Ductility means capable of being drawn out or hammered thin, easily led or influenced, capable of being fashioned into a new form. This is where we get to see the actual transformation taking place, and why the heat and the hardness in our lives have been so intense. We are being pounded on; therefore, we are greatly influenced to take on our new form. A hammer is to hit what is hard, to make the object take a different shape (Jer. 23:29).

When it comes to a hard metal, there is a formula that's quite effective for extracting various contaminants and impurities from it. A drawing out if you will. The two components that make up this procedure are a Fiery Heat and The Duration of Time. When the vessel is placed in the furnace, the fire is brought to the specified temperature and held in this heat for the required amount of time. Once the vessel has been placed in the line of fire, so to speak, the heat surrounds the vessel and maintains its intensity of heat until penetration to the inside has occurred. Once the metal has completely softened, it lets go of its impurities. The heat then draws out the undesirables, or contaminants and brings them to the surface. This is called "Soaking the Metal." This stage changes the internal structure of the metal. Once this has been accomplished, the vessel must go through a slow cooling process. A slow cooling speed is important in order to avoid tensions caused by temperature differences in the metal. When the metal has cooled, the contaminants are removed. The vessel has become pure, strong, and free from all that was causing the internal stresses. At this point, the vessel has a better chance of not cracking under external stresses that it will face during its operation in the field.

It's an internal stress for the heart to hold onto bitterness and unforgiveness. These are impurities that contaminate and weaken the vessel. When the heart suffers the blows of what it perceives to be a violation, it grabs the offense and tucks it away in the memory bank, so as to protect itself against future atrocities.

In the heart's refusal to forgive the offense, it will recall the offense over and over, branding the memory, while making demands for the payment of injustice. This behavior is creating internal stresses that are alive and active that literally bring about an internal breakdown, which in time will manifest through various behaviors. When the offense is locked in a hard heart, intense heat is required to soften the heart long enough to pull the contamination out, so the heart can be relieved.

Again, the purpose for the fiery trials in our lives is to purge hidden wickedness. To purge means to free from moral defilement; also, it is the removal of elements or members regarded as undesirable, treacherous or disloyal. Have you ever noticed how our elder brothers and sisters in the Lord can endure their trials in a smoother fashion while abiding in a restful and peaceful state? I have surmised that these are the beautiful results of the stress relieving fires.

My precious one, forget those things which are behind, so you can move forward; then, cast down the thoughts and imaginations that do not line up with God's Word. The Lord Jesus will help you. Forget all the little details of the offense, so you can walk in and towards forgiveness. If you will practice keeping your mind on Jesus, then He will keep you in peace. A perfect peace. Trust me, if you will apply this, you will be amazed at the results.

> *Brethren, I count not myself to have*
> *apprehended: but this one thing I do,*
> *forgetting those things which are behind,*
> *and reaching forth unto those things which*
> *are before, I press toward the mark for*
> *the prize of the high calling of*
> *God in Christ Jesus.*
> *(Phil. 3:13-14)*

> *Casting down imaginations,*
> *and every High thing that exalteth*
> *itself against the knowledge of God,*
> *and bringing into captivity every*
> *thought to the obedience of Christ.*
> *(2 Cor. 10:5)*

> *Thou wilt keep him in perfect peace,*
> *whose mind is stayed on thee:*
> *because he trusteth in thee.*
> *(Isa. 26:3)*

Quenching and Tempering

There is another procedure known as quenching and tempering. This process brings the metal to a critical point of heat, then quickly immerses it in fresh water to achieve a rapid setting of the desired metallurgical structure. The metal needs to cool rapidly to stop the process of change to hold the quality of that metal at the desired level. Right after the quenching process, the metal is quickly placed in a fired furnace for the tempering; this softens the metal's structure to achieve the desired mechanical properties in the metal.

Have you ever got so frustrated that you swung your hands in the air and said, "Awe, come on! I can't get out of one fire before I have another one waiting for me!" That's because another fire is waiting for you, precious one. God is working!!!

Quenching is to extinguish the fire or put it out. Tempering the metal is to reheat the metal again, but at a lower temperature for further adjustments. The reheating process deals with the qualities in the metal by bringing balance. The actual purpose for the tempering process is to make the vessel stronger and more resilient through hardship. The Lord has told us in the Scriptures that once He begins a good work, He will continue this work until Jesus Christ returns (Phil.1:6). Here is another scripture that is fitting:

*Beloved, think it not strange concerning the
fiery trial which is to try you, as though some
strange thing happened unto you. But rejoice
in as much as ye are partakers of Christ's
sufferings; that when His Glory shall be
revealed, ye may be glad also with
exceeding joy.
(1 Peter 4:12)*

If our vessel has not been purged of its impurities and
made solid inside and out, we will crack under pressure. We
will not be able to deal with the hardships once we are placed
in the field for operation. Our time in the furnace is of the
utmost importance. Our human vessel has been
contaminated with the perversion of sin, and must be
changed because it is deadly. Easy living is dangerous and
brings no change.

*Moab hath been at ease from his youth;
he hath settled on his lees, and hath not
been emptied from vessel to vessel, neither
hath he gone into captivity: therefore his
taste remained in him, and his scent is not
changed.
(Jer. 48:11)*

Our scent needs to change!!!

Let's look at a few Scriptures having to do with the furnace.

For they be thy people, and thine inheritance,
which thou broughtest forth out of Egypt,
from the midst of the furnace of iron.
(1Kings 8:51)

Behold I have refined thee, but not with
silver; I have chosen thee in the furnace
of affliction.
(Isa.48:10)

Behold I created the smith that bloweth
the coals in the fire, and that bringeth forth
an instrument for his work; and I have
created the waster to destroy.
(Isa.54:16)

Which I commanded your fathers in the day
that I brought them forth out of the land of
Egypt, from the iron furnace, saying, obey
My voice, and do them, according to all
which I command you: so, shall ye be
My people, and I will be your God.
(Jer.11:4)

The fining pot is for silver, and the
furnace for gold: but the Lord trieth
the hearts.
(Prov.17:3)

But He knoweth the way that I take:
when He hath tried me, I shall come
forth as gold.
(Job 23:10)

Wherein ye greatly rejoice, though now
for a season, if need be, ye are in
heaviness through manifold temptations.
That the trial of your Faith, being much
more precious than of gold that perisheth,
though it be tried with fire, might be found
unto Praise and Honor and Glory at the
appearing of Jesus Christ.
(1Peter 1:6-7)

I found it interesting that God referred to Egypt as a furnace for His people. Which said to me, that our days of being in Egypt have also been our furnace. I have for some years felt a kinship with our brother, Job, and referred to his trial many times for comfort. His time in the furnace was like no other. I would like for us to study a portion of it. Here we will see how Job handles his fiery trial in the furnace of affliction.

Behold, I go forward, but he is not there;
and backward, but I cannot perceive Him:
On the left hand, where he doth work,
but I cannot behold Him; he hideth himself
on the right hand, that I cannot see him:
But he knoweth the way that I take: when he
hath tried me, I shall come forth as gold.
(Job 23:8-10)

My foot hath held his steps, his way
have I kept, and not declined. Neither
have I gone back from the Commandment
of his lips: I have esteemed the Words
of his mouth more than my necessary
food. But he is in one mind, and who
can turn him? And what his soul desires,
even that he doeth.
(Job 23:11-13)

For he performeth the thing that is
appointed for me: and many such
things are with him. Therefore, am I
troubled at his Presence: When I consider,
I am afraid of him. For God maketh my
heart soft, and the Almighty troubles
me. Because I was not cut off before
the darkness, neither hath he covered
the darkness from my face.
(Job 23:14-17)

Job is relentlessly searching for God in his hour of darkness and does not understand the whys. However, he does know that God is having His way, which is always a comfort to know God is with us, even though we cannot see Him. So, hold on my dear friend. We may not see, but God can.

Chapter Seven

Examined and Tested

The spirit of man is the candle of the Lord, searching all the inward parts of the belly. (Prob. 20:27)

Under the Light

After the vessel has been looked over at the check-out phase, it is released to undergo a random examination of the welded seams to see if the metals merged properly.

There is a procedure and a test called Radiography Testing (RT). This test is comparable to a doctor taking an x-ray of an arm to determine if a bone has been broken or cracked in some way. X-ray technology utilizes high energy rays that can pass through an object. The photons of the beam reach the film causing a chemical reaction which produces an image. The examiner joins the image with light making the results visible for study. This reminds me of how the Lord will examine us.

X-raying a seam where the metals have been joined, is to detect any cracks or lack of fusion. If the examiner locates anything of the sort, the vessel is sent back to the shop; the seam is cut out, and the process of joining the metals start over again. If the fusion of the metals were found to be solid throughout the entire seam, then the vessel has passed the examination and is ready for the next phase.

Tested by Water

Another test, commonly referred to as Hydro-testing, is to see if the vessel can endure pressure without cracking.

After the fabricated vessel has passed all previous testings, it is then brought to a set of jack stands to see if it can pass the test of pressure. The fellows start by capping all open ends, except one, so there is no vent or way of escape. A water hose is attached to the open, threaded end of a valve, which is attached to the piece being tested. The vessel is then filled with water to full capacity. A pressure machine is attached and the psi (pounds per square inch) is brought to the specified rating and held for the required duration of time. Usually, it's around 2500 psi for about 10 minutes.

The high pressure behind the water is for the purpose of forcing the water through any possible holes or cracks to see if the joining metals have been fused properly. If there are no leaks to be found at any point, the vessel is solid through and through and is able to handle pressure without cracking and leaking water. If water is found leaking from the vessel anywhere, this indicates lack of fusion and is a point of weakness. The vessel is brought back to the shop for additional work on the area of weakness. After the work has been completed, the vessel is brought back to the workstation for another test of pressure.

It is interesting to note that the test of pressure did not come until after the vessel was filled to full capacity. Have you ever noticed how your life can be filled to full capacity, so much so that you can hardly take one more thing on your plate? Then the next thing you know, you are beginning to feel a great deal of pressure? On top of it all, you arrive home to find your child is late for practice, so you jump back in the car and head that way. Ten minutes before you turn into the ball field your engine catches on fire. Pulling over as fast as you can, your tire unravels and blows off the rim. Finally, coming to a stop, so you can breathe, your teenager in the back seat whispers a suggestion for your dilemma to remind you that they still have all the answers, and you blow! This would be a leak in the vessel, and another round in the shop may be required -backed by another pressure test, of course!

Polished and Ready

Now that the vessel has been fabricated and tested, it is time for the cleaning and polishing stage. This will be the last phase the vessel goes through at the shop before it is sent to the field.

As the vessel was in the making and enduring the process of change, it got dirty. At every joint and seam, there is a discoloration due to oxidation. With the mixture of oxygen, argon and heat, the metal has been tarnished. An acid-based cleaning agent is used along with a polishing rag to do away with the discoloration in the metal and bring it back to a lustrous shine.

One day the fellows needed an extra hand, and I was not busy. I put some gloves on and made my way over to clean the seams of a big stainless-steel piece. They said, "Wendy, be careful this cleaner is an acid, and wherever it touches on you, it will burn. It will even burn a hole right through your clothes."

By the time I finished helping the men folk, my hair was smoking, and I looked like I had just walked through a bed of piranhas. I had holes everywhere in my clothes and burn marks on my arms. I thought, "Gee whiz, no wonder that metal is shining. That tarnished color was burned out." Needless to say, the fellows had a good laugh.

Now that the vessel is good and clean, the last inspection from the Quality Control department is done to make sure the vessel is up to standard. Once satisfied, the piece is loaded onto the truck and brought to the field. The plan will be looked at again to see where the vessel will be set up for operation.

There is very little to look at as we are going from station to station for another phase of being worked on. However, certain aspects of beauty in the vessel and their potential are evident, but for the most part, it's an ugly sight to watch what comes from a wicked heart as it's being worked on. God really knows how to work on us and get us ready for the field. I have seen three tools in operation. The Hammer, The Fire, and The Knife.

Is not My Word like as a fire?
saith the Lord; and like a hammer
that breaketh the rock in pieces?
(Jer.23:29)

At that time the Lord said unto Joshua,
make thee sharp knives, and
circumcise again the children of
Israel the second time.
(Joshua 5:2)

At times, we have endured the burn of fire in our hearts when we were confronted with a hard truth. At other times we have encountered a hard-repetitive message we don't want to hear, until we say, "Every time so and so comes around, they start that preaching, and I feel like I am being hammered." This is because God's word is the Hammer that breaks to pieces the hardness in our lives, so His Truth can penetrate our lives and bring us to a place of freedom. The person is not the hammer - The Word is. Again, we have experienced the sharp knife of God as He separates us unto Himself.

All these tools are painful. So, as we are being worked on, we become discolored. This will cause various attitudes of the heart to manifest which can tarnish our reputation. Working on a vessel is dirty work because impurities and contaminants are dirty. Therefore, the tarnished areas of our lives are not so appealing. Be encouraged, my precious one because once all the work has been done, and we are ready for the field, God has a cleaning agent that can wipe away the tarnish from our metal, and a rag that can polish us to a shine.

Chapter Eight

Vessels in the Field

**But in a great house there are not only
Vessels of gold and of silver, but also
Of wood and of earth; and some to
Honour, and some to dishonour.
(2 Tim. 2:20)**

There are many vessels that are operating in the field, and each one has been made for a particular use. A vessel is simply a container for holding something. We have a glass container to hold our water, a bowl for our soup, storage containers for miscellaneous items. We have a vessel that allows us to enjoy a nice warm bath known as our hot water heater. There are marine vessels (ships, boats, and submarines) designed to provide transportation across water. We have tiny vessels that run throughout our body to transport our blood. Our body itself is a container or vessel, which holds our soul, spirit, and internal workings.

As we can see, not all vessels are the same. All vessels are different and have their place for a reason. No container is ever made without first having a purpose. The substance already exists. A container just needs to be made to hold it. Man did not create water, that already existed; but, we have learned how to make the cups to hold it. King David revealed an amazing truth found in the book of Psalms.

> *My substance was not hid from thee, when*
> *I was made in secret, and curiously*
> *wrought in the lowest parts of the*
> *Earth. Thine eyes did see my substance,*
> *yet being unperfect; and in thy book all my*
> *members were written, which in*
> *continuance were fashioned, when as yet*
> *there was none of them.*
> *(Ps.139:15-16)*

Digester Vessel

Let's have a look at some interesting vessels and their purpose in the piping industry and how they can shed some light on us human vessels out here working in the field.

There is a vessel known as the digester vessel. The digester is an interesting contraption that behaves much like our digestive system which acts to break down a product. From a spiritual standpoint, have you ever encountered someone who goes against the popular flow by bringing down various mindsets or wrong belief systems that tend to get built up in our lives? Have you ever encountered someone who stood against something, that had the potential to harm you?

Looking through the Scriptures, we find such a man used in a similar fashion. I speak of the vessel, Jeremiah. After God reveals to him that He has made him to be a prophet, we see a dialog spring into action at the rebuttal of Jeremiah's fear. Let's listen in on a portion of their conversation that we may learn how God works with a vessel that He has created, and how this vessel is to be used. Our privilege to have a front row seat to this action is found in the book of Jeremiah.

> *Before I formed thee in the belly, I knew*
> *thee; and before thou camest forth out*
> *of the womb I sanctified thee, and I ordained*
> *thee a Prophet unto the nations. Ah,*
> *Lord God! Behold, I cannot speak: for I*
> *am a child. Say not, I am a child: for*
> *thou shalt go to all that I shall send thee,*
> *and whatsoever I command thee thou*
> *shalt speak. Be not afraid of their faces:*
> *for I am with thee to deliver thee. Then the*
> *Lord put forth His Hand and touched*
> *my mouth. And the Lord said unto me,*
> *Behold, I have put My Words in thy mouth.*
> *See I have this day set thee over the nations*
> *and over the kingdoms, to root out,*
> *and to pull down, and to destroy,*
> *and to throw down, to build, and to plant.*
> *(Jer. 1:5-10)*

My! My! The Lord was about to clean house down here by giving Jeremiah four ways to operate towards the destructive side and only two ways towards the constructive side. Let's continue so we can see how God tested His vessel before He used him.

> *Moreover, the Word of the Lord came unto*
> *me saying, Jeremiah, what seest thou? I see*
> *a rod of an almond tree. Thou hast well seen:*
> *for I will hasten My Word to perform it.*
> *(Jer. 1:11-12)*

Jeremiah passes God's test regarding his sight, but another one is right behind it.

> *And the Word of the Lord came unto me*
> *the second time, saying, What seest thou?*
> *And I said, I see a seething pot; and the*
> *face thereof is toward the north.*
> *(Jer. 1:13)*

Seeing that Jeremiah was able to see properly, God wasted no time in cranking Jeremiah's motor for operation. In verses 14-16, God reveals to His prophet that He is about to move against the people in judgment due to forsaking Him and worshiping other gods. The Lord deals with Jeremiah directly by instructing and preparing him for what was to come.

*Thou therefore gird up thy loins, and arise,
and speak unto them all that I command thee;
be not dismayed at their faces, lest I
confound thee before them. For, behold,
I have made thee this day a defensed city,
and an iron pillar, and brasen walls
against the whole land, against the kings
of Judah, against the princes thereof,
against the Priests thereof, and against
the people of the land. And they shall
fight against thee; but they shall not prevail
against thee; for I am with thee,
says the Lord, to deliver thee.
(Jer. 1:17-19)*

First, we learn that God knew Jeremiah, sanctified and ordained him, and all of this took place before he was even born. This vessel was in the making to contain a substance that already existed: God's Word! God's Word was in existence from the beginning, and before mankind was ever created. After God created Jeremiah, He filled him with His Word. After He filled him, He tested him. After He tested him, He put him in the field.

Process Vessel

The process vessel, as it is called, is used to complete a process that requires pressure to perform a task. Have you ever had your boss come to your desk to ask you where you are at on a job? And we respond by showing him what's been done thus far, and what we have left to do. After recognition of our progress, we are encouraged to remember the dead line.

This is the operation of the process vessel. The employee is in the process of working out a task. The boss is then used to come in and add the necessary pressure to keep us in performance mode. The boss is the pressure vessel, which we will look at later. When we become exhausted and tempted to throw in the towel, certain pressures or pressure vessels are moved in on us to make us get up and continue until the job has been completed. This vessel can come in the form of a parent baring down on their child to finish their chores, or again a boss who applies pressure to get a job done. These vessels are about as popular as our brother, Jeremiah, and they are usually people placed in a position of authority.

Heat Exchanger Vessel

Moving right along, to have a look at another vessel known as the Heat Exchanger Vessel. This particular one is used to add or remove heat. Heat actually means the transfer of energy.

Have you ever noticed that a person can be put in your life and the heat gets turned up, and when they are gone, the heat is removed? Scenario; You have worked all day, being pulled in every direction. Your boss calls you in his office with a complaint from a jealous co-worker.

You're finally able to sit down for your lunch break, when the teacher calls, because your child wants to test the waters. So as the pressure continues to build and your head is about to blow off your shoulders, your next-door neighbor calls to inform you that Fluffy has eaten a hole in your new couch. Exhausted and reaching for the time clock, this same co-worker engages you in a confrontation, so instead of settling down in your recliner with a good book, you drive 90 miles an hour to get home, just so you can clean out the garage. The heat of the day was a transference of energy that woke you up long enough to get the garage clean. If a husband does something to fire his wife up, he can have a clean house in about seven minutes. I don't know how much I would suggest this due to the aftermath. Nevertheless, heat does pass energy to us.

I am reminded of another house cleaning that took place through an exchange of heat found in the book of John involving Jesus and the Jew's Passover. Let's watch how Jesus cleans a house.

> *And the Jews' Passover was at hand, and*
> *Jesus went up to Jerusalem, and found*
> *in the Temple those who sold oxen*
> *and sheep and doves, and the changers of*
> *money sitting: and when He had made a*
> *scourge of small cords, He drove them all*
> *out of the Temple, and the sheep, and the oxen;*
> *and poured out the changers money, and*
> *overthrew the tables; And said unto them*
> *who sold doves, take these things hence;*
> *make not My Father's house an house of*

*merchandise. And His disciples remembered
that it was written, the zeal of thine
house has eaten Me up.
(John 2:13-17)*

My Heavens, now this was an exchange of heat.
When Jesus saw what was going on, He grew hot, braided a
whip and cleaned house. I don't know about anybody else,
but if Jesus walked up and took time to braid a whip in front
of me, I would remove myself.

Pressure Vessel

Moving on to the Pressure Vessel. This is a common
vessel that most all of us are familiar with. Pressure vessels,
of course, are built to handle pressure. Each one of us has
been around someone who has to handle a great deal of
pressure. Mostly I have seen this vessel placed in a position
of authority, as well. These types of individuals are not
always easy to be around. The demands on their life and
position can be extremely heavy, and they seem to be pulled
on from every direction. It is always best to remain light
footed around these particular vessels, for obvious reasons.

Looking at the Pressure Vessels that are used in the
industry gives us a little insight into this vessel's nature. The
Pressure Vessel is a specialized vessel used anytime a
substance is under either internal, or external pressure, or
both. It is a closed container designed to hold gases or liquids
at a high pressure. It is imperative for this vessel to have a

proper relief system, for the sake of enduring pressure. These vessels are known for supporting entire operating systems in the field. People who work with pressure vessels on a regular basis are required to have a specific training and knowledge due to the vessel's potentially hazardous nature. One of the phases of training is how to handle the pressurized container carefully, so as to prevent a possible explosion and setting everything on fire.

These vessels are powerful and serve a great purpose, and the pressure they contain is serious. If a pressurized vessel should ever crack and leak, this can be volatile. If the crack becomes large enough, it can seriously weaken the vessel, and it will explode causing a reaction of fire. Due to their nature and purpose, they are required to endure a rigid quality control process.

When we are around people who have serious natures, it is because they are containing something serious. These natures are of a heavy weight class and are pressurized with a powerful way about them. They are not usually soft and cuddly - but bold, revered and respected. Pressure Vessels are made to house and hold flammable gases under pressure. One could say that this vessel contains a fiery nature. A wrong move can cause us to get burned. We enjoy the benefits of a service station, so we can put gas in our cars, but let someone carelessly throw a lite match around this gas containing vessel, and it's a run for your life situation. We appreciate our flammable services; however, we are also wise to have a healthy respect for their potential.

Proceed with Caution

Looking at the animal kingdom we have seen time after time people raising baby lions, bears and tigers, and how close of a relationship we can have with them. We love them, and they love us. That was never an issue between the care giver and the animal. Besides, the love between them was established when they were just a baby in most cases. So, love itself was never the issue, their nature is the issue.

In my research, I came across a couple of hazardous situations involving pressurized vessel's blowing up in the field. In 1998, a catastrophic situation occurred in Pitkin, Louisiana, in which a pressure vessel blew up and killed four men. Upon investigation, they discovered that the vessel was made to endure more pressure than it was created to handle. On top of this, it was discovered that the vessel had no relief system, and the only vent that was available had been blocked off. With added pressure and no vent, the vessel had to blow.

Another vessel caught the attention of its surrounding neighbors at a local oil and chemical company located in Houston, Texas. In 2004, a 50,000lb pressurized vessel blew. During investigation it was discovered that the vessel had been mishandled by improper welding and unauthorized modifications, thus compromising the vessel. As a result, heavy fragments blew a thousand feet until it struck a nearby building, causing structural damage.

Looking at both catastrophes, we see that one vessel was made to bear more than what it was meant to carry, with no way of relief. The other vessel was mishandled and not cared for in the proper way. I am reminded of how our God is according to scripture. Although our Father loves us very much, He has a powerful nature about Him. The book of Hebrews offers us a glimpse into God's nature.

> *Wherefore, we are receiving a kingdom which cannot be moved, let us have grace, whereby we may serve God acceptably with reverence and godly fear. For our God is a consuming fire.*
> *(Heb. 12:28-29)*

Even our Lord God has a nature of fire. Just one of many examples of God's fiery nature and what He thinks about being mishandled is found in Leviticus:

> *Then Nadab and Abihu, the sons of Aaron, took either of them his censer, and put fire therein, and put incense thereon, and offered strange fire before the Lord, which He commanded them not. And there went out fire from the Lord, and devoured them, and they died before the Lord. Then Moses said unto Aaron, "This is it that the Lord spake, saying, "I will be sanctified in them that come nigh me, and before all the people I will be glorified." And Aaron held his peace.*
> *(Lev. 10:1-3)*

I do not know the impact this has on anyone else. As for me, if I saw two people drop dead in front of me, then I would acquire a reverential fear for the Lord before I decided to inhale my next breath. I would then educate myself in whatever way necessary to ensure that my dealings with the Lord met His standards.

The fear of the Lord is the beginning of wisdom:
and the knowledge of the holy is understanding.
(Prov. 9:10)

Nuclear Powered Vessel

There is another vessel referred to as the "Nuclear Powered Vessel." This one fascinates me. This amazing vessel houses a system of operations involving water, pressure and heat in which passes through a chain of reactors to produce power. Nuclear power is also used to sustain and empower the vessel for a long period of time before having to refuel.

This reminds me of the life empowered by the Holy Spirit. As our younger generation is approaching the world scene, I am seeing some Nuclear-Powered vessels who are on fire for God. We have a few Nuclear-Powered vessels found in the Scriptures. However, there is one vessel, in particular, that I have always been intrigued with, who walked in power and encountered a Nuclear-Powered situation involving water, pressure and heat - Elijah! Approaching God's Word to see this incredible scene found in 1Kings 18:17-39, we see that God had enough of the false gods and false prophets, so He sets the fuel to Elijah with the intent of dealing with the situation.

Elijah sets off a chain of reactors by sending word to gather all of Israel and 850 false prophets, (450 prophets of Baal and 400 prophets of Asherah.) Elijah then steps in the ring with a bold and powerful word, "How long halt ye between two opinions? If the Lord be God, follow Him: but if Baal, then follow him."

Here we have one man standing in front of all Israel and staring into the faces of 850 lying prophets. I would venture to say that we have indeed located the pressurized portion of this Nuclear-Powered situation. Let us continue in our journey until we find the water!!!

Contending with the people, Elijah presents a challenge to the 450 prophets of Baal for the express purpose of proving who the real God is. Elijah's challenge involved a sacrifice!

Let them therefore give us two bullocks;
and let them choose one bullock for
themselves, and cut it in pieces, and
lay it on wood, and put no fire under:
and I will dress the other bullock, and lay
it on wood, and put no fire under: And
call ye on the name of your gods, and I
will call on the name of the Lord; and the
God that answereth by fire, let Him be God.
(1King 18:23-24)

Notice how Elijah even lets them have first choice of the bulls. After the false prophets prepared the sacrifice on the altar, they began calling on their god, Baal. They continued from morning until noon, but there was no answer. They even leaped upon the altar. As we continue through the scriptures, we see Elijah making fun of their god, saying,

> *"Cry aloud: for he is a god, either he is talking, or he is pursuing, or he is in a journey, or peradventure he sleepeth, and must be awakened."*
> *(1 Kings 18:27)*

Elijah's words of fuel sparked an outrageous display of crying aloud and cutting themselves. The Bible records it this way.

> *And they cried aloud, and cut Themselves after their manner with knives and lancets, till the blood gushed out upon them. And it came to pass, when midday was past, and they prophesied until the time of the offering of the evening sacrifice, that there was neither voice, nor any to answer, nor any that regarded.*
> *(1 Kings 18: 28-29)*

Here we see how Elijah lets the false prophets have first choice: he lets them go first; and, then, gives them the better part of the day to convince all that their false god, Baal had no power. Elijah then ends this foolish display, by instructing the people to draw near. He then sets the stage for God to demonstrate His power that all may know who the real God is. After the people moved in closer, Elijah begins by preparing a broken-down altar, that was the Lords. Then he took twelve stones which represented the twelve tribes of Israel.

With these stones, Elijah built an altar to the Lord for his sacrifice. Then he dug a trench around the altar. He put the wood in order, cut the bull to pieces, and then laid him on the wood. Here comes our water we need for our Nuclear situation!!!

After laying his sacrifice on the wood, Elijah gives instruction to fill four barrels with water, and pour it on the sacrifice, and on the wood. After this, Elijah said, "Do it again." When they did as they were instructed, Elijah said, "Do it again." Three times Elijah makes a request for four barrels of water - which totaled twelve barrels of water. Everything Elijah is being made to do in this situation has real significance.

Looking at the twelve stones and twelve barrels of water makes for an interesting study. According to E.W. Bullinger's book entitled "Number in Scripture," his first quote in reference to the number twelve says this, "Twelve is a perfect number, signifying "Perfection of Government, or of Governmental perfection." It is found as a multiple in all that has to do with rule."

So simply put **"God Rules!!!"**

As we continue through our journey with Elijah, we locate our element of heat in 1Kings 18:36-39. Looking at this incredible amount of water, we see that Elijah made it absolutely impossible for fire to burn on his altar and sacrifice. Nevertheless, Elijah lifted his voice and said:

Lord God of Abraham, Isaac and of Israel, let it be known this day that thou art God in Israel, and that I am thy servant, and that I have done all these things at thy word. Hear me, O' Lord, hear me, that this people may know that thou art the Lord God, and that thou hast turned their heart back again.
(1 Kings 18:36-37)

Then the fire of the Lord fell, and consumed the burnt sacrifice, and the wood, and the stones, and the dust, and licked up the water that was in the trench. And when all the people saw it, they fell on their faces; and they said, "The Lord, he is the God, the Lord, he is the God.
(1 Kings 18:38-39)

After this, Elijah had all the false prophets gathered together and put them to death. The Scriptures reveal that Elijah was used in sixteen miracles, thus making him no stranger to the power of God. After a life of walking in this kind of power, God sends a chariot of fire with horses of fire and snatches Elijah off the earth, bringing him home (2 Kings 2:11). Elijah was a Nuclear-Powered Vessel!!

A Personal Note:

My friend, whatever God has built us for, let us operate in this, and not extend ourselves beyond the limits God has set for us, according to Paul's exhortation found in 2 Cor. 10:13-16. Please know how valuable you are to the rest of us vessels out here working. Know well that you are very much needed and serve a tremendous purpose. It is good to let God have His way in our lives because only He knows what He has built us for. The Lord knows the specific trials He has allowed for our training and building. He knows where to position us in the field for operation. He knows where we fit best.

Let us have mercy one toward another knowing that we are all built and fashioned in a diverse manner for a specific task. Also, let us not desire the place or position of another, but be content with what the Lord has been gracious to give us. A rightful place is a beautiful operation. If we purpose in our hearts to fit in a position we have not been built for, an obstruction in the flow will take place and bring discontentment to every vessel working until the right person is found. There are many reasons one would try to force themselves in a position they were not built for. Mostly, I have seen money as the predominate reason for this. However, if money be the ruler that dictates our position in life, then we will endure pressures we were not designed to bare, and we will not know peace.

Following the ways of the world will lead us to a place of frustration with no rest, following Jesus Christ will lead us to green pastures, still waters, restoration of soul and paths of righteousness (Psalm 23:1-3). How sweet it is to follow someone who really knows where they are going. Remember, my dear brothers and sisters, when you become weary from working in the field, shut all operations down. Go to The Fountain and stand in His Light until you are nourished by the Living Waters. Let us pray!

Now, Lord Jesus,

Help us to lay aside our own understanding, deny what we think is right, and pick up our cross. That we may follow You, as You lead us to our place of operation in this world. That we may learn to serve You in the fullness of what You have designed us for. Lord, when You look upon our lives as we function in our daily activities, may Your face be brightened with pleasure. May You receive the full Glory as Your power to redeem a man is manifested in our lives. In the name of Jesus Christ, the Fountain of Living Waters, I pray. Amen!!!

Your Tambourine Player,

Wendy Winans

One Last Thing

One last thing before you go! Do you remember the testimony I
shared pertaining to the Mother who lost her children? And how I asked the
Lord, "Will I too become gray headed before I see my children?"
Well, that answer was "Yes."
So, I have opted to save
one last review for
this book till the
end. Reading
"A Vessel
Made
Ready" and
seeing the beauty
that can come from the
trials my mother has gone
through is simply amazing! This is
such a timely message to not lose hope
when we are going through difficult situations
and to put our eyes on Jesus. The best part of this
book is not only gaining understanding of the process,
but to see how God builds us into the vessels we need
to be. That we may fulfill our calling in life. Through this
work I can see that my mother leads us back to the Bible
and the One who has all the answers we're searching for.
Jesus! I'm living proof of how God can restore and bring
healing from life's most difficult trials. The Lord has
brought my mother and I back together after 20
years and is continuing to restore to us the
time lost. So, thank you Mom for being
obedient to the Lord in writing "A
Vessel Made Ready" and
teaching us what the
Lord has taught
you so,
we may not
lose hope when hard times come.

Brittany Norris
Entrepreneur / Evangelist
Baton Rouge, La

Made in the USA
Monee, IL
03 November 2020